Divine Generosity

Divine Generosity

THE SCOPE OF SALVATION
IN REFORMED THEOLOGY

Richard J. Mouw

WILLIAM B. EERDMANS PUBLISHING COMPANY
GRAND RAPIDS, MICHIGAN

Wm. B. Eerdmans Publishing Co.
4035 Park East Court SE, Grand Rapids, Michigan 49546
www.eerdmans.com

Book design by Leah Luyk

Printed in the United States of America

30 29 28 27 26 25 24   1 2 3 4 5 6 7

ISBN 978-0-8028-8390-2

Library of Congress Cataloging-in-Publication Data

A catalog record for this book is available from the Library of
Congress.

To Margriet and Kees van der Kooi

You have had a significant influence
on a gifted group
—more than a dozen in number—
of Fuller Seminary neo-Calvinist doctoral students.
Both through theological teaching
and in practical acts of hospitality
you have pointed all of us
to the abundant grace
of a generous God.

Contents

Acknowledgments

AT VARIOUS POINTS during my writing this book I showed drafts to some friends: Jon Balserak, Jessica Joustra, Suzanne McDonald, Sam Logan, and Barbara Wheeler. I knew that each of them shared my desire to portray Calvinism as a more generous theological system, and I wanted them to tell me if I was making the case effectively. Each of them urged me to keep on with the project, and I am grateful to them for much-needed words of encouragement. I also want to thank Nick Barrett for producing the index.

1

Rejecting Universalism

I AM NOT A UNIVERSALIST. There is nothing surprising about my saying that. Having spent my career in evangelical institutions, I have signed many theological statements affirming the realities of heaven and hell, and I have always done so in good faith.

But here is something that would surprise many of my fellow evangelicals: I don't even *want to be* a universalist. I have heard this fairly often in evangelical conversations: "I would like to be a universalist, but I really see no biblical basis for the view that everyone will be saved in the end." I have not argued with those who express that sentiment, but I have privately dissented because I do not want to come across as someone who takes delight in the idea of unbelievers going to hell. I do believe, however, that the idea of universal salvation fails to capture some important elements in the Bible's teachings about the requirements of divine justice.

I was pleased to discover that N. T. Wright makes the kind of case that I think needs to be made, in his *Surprised by Hope.* Wright is particularly upset with "the cheap and cheerful uni-

---

This chapter first appeared in a different form in the February 13, 2023, edition of *Christianity Today*, under the title "I Don't Want to Be a Universalist."

versalism of Western liberalism." He rightly acknowledges—as I do —that there are more serious and nuanced efforts in Christian history to defend universalism. For himself, though, he confesses that he finds it impossible to accept universalism as he studies "the New Testament on the one hand and the newspaper on the other." Accounts of "the murder of children and the careless greed that enslaves millions with debts not their own" cry out for the "ultimate condemnation" of those who willfully perpetrate such cruelties.[1] Wright is insisting here that we take seriously the need for a decisive end-time accounting for the grave injustices that occur in our world. In our understandable reluctance to sound like we want people to experience an ultimate condemnation, we often fail to pay adequate attention to the cries of justice that come from the victims of oppression.

It will be clear in what I argue in this book that while I have fairly strong objections to universalist theology, I also want to encourage the idea of a more generous distribution of God's saving mercies, as a counter to the restrictive "small number of the elect" conception often associated with Calvinism. It is important for me at the beginning, then, to make it clear that my desire for a more generous theology is in no way motivated by universalist sympathies.

The Hitler Case

In his recent book defending universalism, *That All Shall Be Saved: Heaven, Hell, and Universal Salvation*, David Bentley Hart discourages us from paying attention to biblical specifics

---

1. N. T. Wright, *Surprised by Hope: Rethinking Heaven, the Resurrection, and the Mission of the Church* (San Francisco: HarperOne, 2008), 180.

in dealing with the topic. All that the Bible provides, he tells us, is "a number of fragmentary and fantastic images that can be taken in any number of ways, arranged according to our prejudices and expectations, and declared literal or figural or hyperbolic as our desires dictate."[2] Instead, Hart argues, we have to ask whether a proper understanding of human nature allows us to believe that "the defiant rejection of God for all eternity is really logically possible for any rational being."[3]

There have been many advocates for universalism who have—unlike Hart—worked hard to square their convictions with the biblical data. I respect those efforts, even though they do not convince me. I was disappointed with Hart's quick and cavalier refusal to consider biblical passages, especially since a couple of my evangelical friends recommended Hart to me as "worth considering" and "fascinating." Most important, though, the Bible clearly contradicts Hart's insistence that a defiant and unrelenting rejection of God's mercies is impossible. Certainly the example of Adolf Hitler looms large in this regard. Haven't the monstrous deeds for which Hitler is responsible put him eternally beyond any claim to God's mercy?

Hart directly addresses the Hitler case. No human being could ever willfully choose, Hart says, to "fulfill the criteria necessary justly to damn himself or herself to perpetual misery." The fact is that "the character of even the very worst among us is in part the product of external contingencies." We have to assume that "somewhere in the history of every soul there are moments when a better way was missed by mischance, or by malign interventions from without, or by disorders of the

---

2. David Bentley Hart, *That All Shall Be Saved: Heaven, Hell, and Universal Salvation* (New Haven: Yale University Press, 2019), 93.

3. Hart, *That All Shall Be Saved*, 17.

mind within."[4] And then, to underscore the point he is making, Hart observes that "rather than any intentional perversity on the soul's own part," these are precisely the kinds of factors at work in a case like Hitler's. The nature of Hitler's deeds, which is surely "infinitely evil in every objective sense," is still "aboriginally prompted into action by a hunger for the Good, [and] could never in perfect clarity of mind match the sheer nihilistic scope of the evil" that resulted from Hitler's deeds. The fact that Hitler was prompted in his actions by "a hunger for the Good," though, means that he "could not rationally resist the love of God willfully for eternity."[5]

Hart tells us that he is drawing upon insights here from several "Christian universalists of the Greek and Syrian east,"[6] and he clearly shares their fondness for Plato's philosophy. Plato taught that since evil is the absence of good, no one willingly chooses that which is evil. This perspective allows Hart to argue that what we might want to label in the Hitler case as "intentional perversity" is in reality a state of ignorance—due to the "external contingencies" that Hart has listed.

Where we might push Hart a bit is on his including the influence of "disorders of the mind within" as one of the factors that could have kept Hitler from clearly grasping the Good. What Hart likely has in mind—in line with his Platonism—are the ways in which some of Hitler's past experiences might have kept him from seeing certain facts clearly. Or maybe Hart thinks that Hitler could not grasp the truth fully because he relied on unreliable sources for his information. Or perhaps he was afflicted with a learning disability.

4. Hart, *That All Shall Be Saved*, 39.

5. Hart, *That All Shall Be Saved*, 40.

6. Hart, *That All Shall Be Saved*, 123.

For those of us who do not want to set the Bible aside in thinking about these matters, we cannot ignore what the apostle Paul says about willful disobedience to the Good: "The wrath of God is being revealed from heaven against all the godlessness and wickedness of people, who suppress the truth by their wickedness, since what may be known about God is plain to them.... [They] are without excuse" (Rom. 1:18–20).[7]

Willful Rebellion

In teaching many courses on Plato's dialogues, I have told my students that this Pauline teaching requires us to reject the Platonistic insistence that it is not possible for a human being to knowingly choose that which is evil. There is, however, a non-Platonistic sense in which the phenomenon of willful rejection of the Good does go against our biblical understanding of human nature. N. T. Wright makes this clear in pointing out that individuals who persistently rebel against God eventually become so dehumanized that they irreparably damage the image of God in which they were created. When they pass on from this life, then, after having "inhabited God's good world, in which the flickering flame of goodness had not been completely snuffed out," they enter into "an ex-human state, no longer reflecting their maker in any meaningful sense." Thus, they have transitioned "not only beyond hope but also beyond pity."[8] Wright reinforces his point by citing C. S. Lewis's observation that in contrast to God's extending his saving mercies to those who

7. Unless otherwise indicated, Scripture quotations are from the New International Version (2011).

8. Wright, *Surprised by Hope*, 182.

have regularly prayed to the Lord, "Thy will be done," in the end God will finally declare to those who have persistently opposed his purposes: "*Thy* will be done."[9]

What Hart's line of argument fails to account for is the fundamentally "directional" character of our spiritual lives. The Westminster Shorter Catechism highlights this factor in its first question and answer, in telling us that our "chief end" as human beings is "to glorify God, and to enjoy him forever."[10] Redeeming grace, then, restores our ability to pursue that "end" once again. We Christians are in a process of moving toward the "end" for which God creates and redeems us. This reality is captured beautifully in 1 John 3:2: "Now we are children of God, and what we will be has not yet been made known. But we know that when Christ appears, we shall be like him, for we shall see him as he is."

In classic theological terms, this is about sanctification as a process and glorification as the goal. When the Spirit plants new life in the deep places of a person's being, the person begins a process of becoming sanctified, moving toward the eschatological goal of being glorified. That end product is "what we will be" when we are brought to our eschatological goal—"when Christ appears."

In the present preglorification stage of our journeys, we live with the mystery of what the fulfillment of our "chief end" will be like. In his "Weight of Glory" essay, C. S. Lewis captures in a memorable way the eschatological mystery of the "doth not yet appear" phenomenon in the Christian journey. Lewis ob-

9. C. S. Lewis, *The Great Divorce: A Dream* (San Francisco: HarperSan-Francisco, 1946), 75.

10. The Westminster Shorter Catechism, Question and Answer 1, in *The Creeds of Christendom, with a History and Critical Notes*, ed. Philip Schaff, vol. 3 (Grand Rapids: Baker Books, 1996), 676.

serves that while each of us has little problem thinking much about our own future glory, we have no problem overdoing our reflection on the future glory of others. It would be spiritually healthy, Lewis says, for us to reverse this pattern: "The load, weight, or burden of my neighbour's glory should be laid daily on my back, a load so heavy that only humility can carry it, and the backs of the proud will be broken." Since we are surrounded by fellow Christians who are "possible gods and goddesses," it is a good spiritual exercise for us to "remember that the dullest and most uninteresting person you talk to may one day be a creature which, if you saw it now, you would be strongly tempted to worship."[11]

This is a compelling observation, and understandably it is frequently cited. But a brief clause that concludes Lewis's observation is less frequently quoted. He immediately adds that in addition to those who will be marvelously glorified, we would witness in some human beings, if we could catch a glimpse of them in *their* final state, "a horror and a corruption such as you now meet, if at all, only in a nightmare."[12] For those who are heading in a direction opposite to that of glorification, it is also true that "it doth not yet appear" what their destination will be like.

The ultimate lost-ness of hell is real. Many of us who affirm that, however, still have questions about who will end up in that state. What about the friendly bank teller who treats each person he serves with genuine kindness—but who is at best a nominal "twice a year" church member? Or the devout Jewish pharmacist who spends several hours a week serving meals at

11. C. S. Lewis, *The Weight of Glory and Other Addresses* (San Francisco: HarperOne, 1976), 45.
12. Lewis, *The Weight of Glory*, 45.

a homeless shelter? Or the Muslim mother in rural Iraq who prays fervently each day that her two children will walk in paths of righteousness?

I wrestle with those kinds of questions, without coming up with clear answers. But I do take comfort in the realization that we can reject universalism while still taking an expansive view of how many will be saved in the end. Here I will take my cue from Charles Spurgeon, who remarked that while the Bible says that "there is to be a multitude that no man can number in heaven," he has not found anything in the Bible that says that "there is to be a multitude that no man can number in hell." The Bible, said Spurgeon, simply does not give us many details about hell.[13]

13. Charles Spurgeon, "Heavenly Worship," the Spurgeon Center, accessed April 5, 2023, sermon on Rev. 14:1–3, preached on December 28, 1856, https://www.spurgeon.org/resource-library/sermons/heavenly-worship/#flipbook/. I owe the reference to Spurgeon on this to William Boekestein, "Are Only Few People Saved?" *Gospel Coalition*, March 13, 2019, https://www.thegospelcoalition.org/article/people-saved/.

2

The Scope of God's Love

ONE OF MY PUBLIC HIGH SCHOOL TEACHERS told us in a class on American literature that Jonathan Edwards was a horrible person. Edwards was a Calvinist preacher, the teacher said, who preached a famous sermon about sinners being punished by an angry God. The teacher told us that he hoped we students would never have to read that sermon. If we did, he said, it would likely give us nightmares.

I decided to risk the nightmares. I was in my midteens, and I had heard the label "Calvinism" used frequently to describe what our kind of Christians believed—I knew it had to do with being "predestined" and having "eternal security." But I had never associated that with a special emphasis on divine anger. So, after school that day, I asked my father, a Reformed pastor, if he knew where I could read a sermon by Jonathan Edwards about an angry Calvinist God. My father took me into his study and pulled an old book from a shelf. It had a promising title: *The Great Sermons of the Great Preachers; or, Masterpieces of Pulpit Eloquence of All Ages and Countries.*

Jonathan Edwards's "Sinners in the Hands of an Angry God" was in the volume, and I did read it. I did not share my teacher's negative reaction. Indeed, it was less likely to give me nightmares than many of the other sermons on hell that I had heard in my youth, particularly from traveling evangelists who warned us of what might soon happen to us if we did not heed their calls to repent of our sins. I could certainly see why this sermon would be included in a volume featuring examples of "pulpit eloquence."

In glancing over the book's table of contents, another sermon caught my eye: "The Small Number of the Saved," preached in the eighteenth century by Jean Baptist Massillon. That title had a Calvinist ring to it, so I read it also. The biblical text was Luke 4:27: "And many lepers were in Israel in the time of Eliseus [Elisha] the prophet; and none of them was cleansed, saving Naaman the Syrian" (KJV). The point of the sermon seemed to fit my understanding of Calvinist teaching, emphasizing that God's redemptive purposes were intended for only a small portion of the human race. It was several years later that I discovered that Massillon was a Jesuit. I still think of him as a Jesuit who preached Calvinist-sounding sermons! I don't remember spending much time thinking about the specific theological issues touched upon in those two sermons. But the few hours that I had spent reading them did give me the sense that Calvinism's way of understanding God's dealings with his human creatures was deserving of respect.

In preparing to write this book, I went back to reread those two sermons. I even read them in the volume where I had first discovered them—my father's copy is long lost, but the book is downloadable online.[1]

1. See https://www.google.com/books/edition/The_great_sermons_of _the_great_preachers/LhwHAAAAQAAJ?hl=en&gbpv=1&dq=The+Great +Sermons+of+the+Great+Preachers%3B+or,+Masterpieces+of+Pulpit+Elo quence+of+all+Ages+and+Countries.&pg=PT2&printsec=frontcover.

They are both excellent sermons. More than six decades removed from that teenage experience, I still find them impressive, and even inspiring at many points. My teenage self was not yet the convinced Calvinist that I have become, and even though I nuance my Calvinist convictions differently these days than how those two preachers proclaimed theirs, I resonate with gratitude to the deep spiritual and theological impulses that are at work in what they say about God's redemptive purposes.

More importantly, in retrospect I see in those sermons emphases on two big topics that have come to dominate my own theological agenda over the years: the character of the Calvinist God, and questions regarding the scope of that God's gracious purposes.

In my thinking about these matters, I have gone in somewhat different theological directions than some of what is set forth in those two sermons. While I certainly do not deny the reality of God's anger against sin, I am strongly inclined to pay a lot of attention to God's love. And in thinking about the "number of the saved," I tend to go with bigger numbers—without, though, slipping into universalism. I'll be giving some attention to that numbers question in later chapters.

Much of my interest in the divine character and related topics has been expressed in my explorations of the proper patterns of a Calvinist ethic based on obedience to divine commands, and more specifically on important topics related to Calvinist engagement in public life. I have also written at length about the nonsalvific workings of "common grace" in the larger human community.

While Calvinist thought boasts significant resources for addressing these broader human concerns, Calvinist theology is widely associated with matters of soteriology, focusing on how a human being gets right with God. And Calvinism certainly does address this topic in a unique voice, with a central emphasis on God's sovereignty. We sinners are totally incapable of effecting our own salvation. The process of getting saved can only happen if God initiates the transaction. We are elected, then, by a sovereign grace that accomplishes unfailingly what God sets out to do. And when God chooses to save a person, that bond cannot be broken by anything in the whole creation. In short, God maintains absolute sovereign control over the process of saving individuals.

What this brief summary makes clear is that Calvinism depicts the human role in the salvific process in passive terms. As the old Calvinist hymn puts it:

> I sought the Lord, and afterward I knew
> he moved my soul to seek him, seeking me.
> It was not I that found, O Savior true,
> no, I was found, was found, of thee.[2]

While I fully endorse that passivity perspective on the salvation of sinners, my theological explorations have focused on those aspects of Calvinism where the *active* voice comes to the fore in the lives of elect people. This happens when we ask what God intends to *bring about in* initiating the process that leads to our salvation. God acts *upon* us, doing for us what we are incapable of doing for ourselves. Once that happens, though, what next? Here we become active, functioning as *agents* of God's purposes in the world. God saves individuals in order to incorporate them into a covenant community that is called to show forth his sovereign rule over all things. Here the Holy Spirit

2. Jean Ingelow, "I Sought the Lord, and Afterward I Knew," Hymnary.org, 1878, https://hymnary.org/text/i_sought_the_lord_and_afterward_i_knew.

works in us, empowering his redeemed people to demonstrate the supreme Lordship of Christ over every sphere of created life. Thus, the ethic of active obedience to divine commands, and our obligation to do our part in fulfilling God's creating and redeeming purposes.

On these "agency" issues, I have aligned myself with the "neo-Calvinist" movement inspired by the theology of cultural engagement developed in the late nineteenth century by the Dutch theologians Abraham Kuyper and Herman Bavinck. Central to this perspective is an insistence that there are God-glorifying thoughts and deeds that occur beyond the boundaries of the redeemed community. This insistence has been spelled out at length in a theology of "common grace," the teaching that there are manifestations of a positive, but nonsaving, attitude of God toward the nonelect, whereby God enlists the talents and virtues of unredeemed people to promote his purposes in the world, in preparation for the coming of the fullness of the kingdom. This kingdom vision, in turn, also takes seriously working for the well-being of the larger human community.

That perspective, however, has not gone unchallenged in the Calvinist world. The Dutch American theologian Cornelius Van Til, for example, argued that while Kuyper and Bavinck set out to develop a consistently Calvinist perspective on the calling of the Christian community, they did not have "the courage to go consistently along the path" of Reformed orthodoxy.[3] Their primary error, Van Til insisted, was overestimating the noetic capacities of the unredeemed human mind, thus undercutting their affirmation of the reality of total depravity.[4] The charge

---

3. Cornelius Van Til, *Common Grace and Witness-Bearing* (Philadelphia: P&R, 1954), 85.

4. Van Til, *Common Grace*, 82–83.

that someone who claims to be a Calvinist downplays the reality of total depravity is a serious one. That doctrine, with a corresponding emphasis on the noetic effects of the Fall, has rightly been seen as a nonnegotiable Calvinist tenet.

Those of us who defend the theology of common grace argue for a distinction between "total" depravity and "absolute" depravity. The latter perspective portrays everything associated with unredeemed life and thought as consistently and fully polluted by sin, whereas for the former perspective, while our shared sinfulness *affects* all areas of human life, manifestations of the good can occur in the lives of the nonelect. These positive thoughts and deeds, however, do not count toward salvation, since our only hope as human beings is to be redeemed by grace alone. The Canons of Dort put the point here clearly, declaring that we are all "by nature children of wrath, incapable of any *saving* good"[5]—thus leaving open the possibility of thoughts and deeds that are morally laudable but not salvifically meritorious.

The distinction here, between that which promotes the good and that which has salvific merit, is one that we find in John Calvin himself. The Reformer frequently argues for a nonsalvific positive attitude that God shows toward nonelect persons. One example that is particularly relevant for present purposes is Calvin's comparison between two public leaders in ancient Rome, Camillus and Catiline. While both men must be seen "under the universal condition of human depravity," he says, there was a significant difference between the two. Catiline engaged in wicked behavior, whereas we can see "endowments resplendent

5. The Canons of the Synod of Dort, Third and Fourth Heads of Doctrine, article 3, in *The Creeds of Christendom, with a History and Critical Notes*, ed. Philip Schaff, vol. 3 (Grand Rapids: Baker Books, 1996), 588.

in Camillus [that] were gifts of God and seem rightly commend-able if judged in themselves." Furthermore, these gifts were "not common gifts of nature, but special graces of God, which he bestows variously and in a certain measure upon men otherwise wicked."[6] But the "graces" here are not salvific. Calvin is clear that while these gifts rightly "have their praise in the political assembly and in common renown among men," they will not be counted in the last judgment as having had any "value to acquire righteousness."[7]

In his account of Calvin's views regarding God's positive assessments of specific deeds performed by the nonelect, Jochem Douma observes that the Reformer also at times refers to a kind of "love" that God shows toward the nonelect.[8]

Not all Calvinists have agreed with Calvin on this. Some simply don't pay theological attention to issues beyond those relating to the standard Calvinist salvation topics. But there are some Calvinist thinkers who actively oppose any notion of a divine love toward anyone outside of the elect community. In my own explorations of common grace theology, I have given serious attention to Calvinist thinkers who simply reject any element of divine favor toward the nonelect. The clearest expression of this outright rejection is found in the writings of theologians in the Protestant Reformed Churches, an ecclesial body founded in 1924 when the Reverend Herman Hoeksema was deposed by the Christian Reformed Church because of

6. John Calvin, *Institutes of the Christian Religion*, ed. John T. McNeill, trans. Ford Lewis Battles, Library of Christian Classics, vols. 20 and 21 (Philadelphia: Westminster, 1960), 2.3.3, p. 293.

7. Calvin, *Institutes* 2.3.4, p. 294.

8. Jochem Douma, *Common Grace in Kuyper, Schilder, and Calvin: Exposition, Comparison, and Evaluation*, ed. William Helder, trans. Albert H. Oosterhoff (Hamilton, ON: Lucerna CRTS, 2017), 247.

his active opposition to the theology of common grace. While Hoeksema was a brilliant theologian, his views are so out of step with mainstream Reformed thought that his theological perspective has been relegated to the margins.

I see that as unfortunate, and I have regularly engaged the views of Hoeksema and his followers. I will do so again here—albeit briefly. While few people in the broader Calvinist community would openly endorse claims associated with a theology that forthrightly opposes common-grace thinking, I am convinced that ideas linked to the Hoeksema perspective do lurk in the background of many attitudes toward culture among Calvinists. Indeed, my sense is that if the many Calvinists who limit their theological attention to soteriological matters were to state explicitly their understanding of "Christ and culture" topics, their views would come close to Hoeksema-type formulations—although without the logical rigor of his efforts.

I have a more personal reason for finding it helpful to engage the Hoeksema perspective. Where his version of Calvinism goes narrow, mine goes broad. This will be obvious as I argue for what I see as a genuinely Calvinist affirmation of salvific generosity. It is important for me to know just where we start going in different directions. We both begin with the fundamental Calvinist affirmation that the only hope for a lost sinner is the sovereign grace that sent the Savior to Calvary. As we begin spelling out our understanding of what that means theologically, though, we begin giving conflicting accounts—and more importantly, we each offer quite different portrayals of the divine character. I want to know where my Calvinism starts going in a different direction from that of many in the Calvinist world. Hoeksema and his colleagues help me to see the issues here clearly.

In spelling out my own views on salvific generosity, though, I take confidence that I am not walking a lonely path.

I will make much here of the fact that my views on the subject are supported—and often with a theological boldness—by a previous generation of theologians whose orthodox Calvinist credentials have been long established: W. G. T. Shedd, Charles Hodge and his son A. A. Hodge, Geerhardus Vos, and Benjamin Warfield. Their views on the extent of God's electing mercies, though, have not been widely discussed. Indeed, in looking into their published writings in recent years, I have been surprised by the tone and substance of their perspective, and I have been forced—happily—to correct what I had previously learned about some of their views from both their admirers and their opponents. An added benefit is that these theologians make their case with careful attention to biblical teaching—and in a manner that inspires wonder at the mysteries of sovereign grace.

Loving the Nonelect

An obvious point where I depart from the Hoeksema perspective is in his endorsement of a positive decree of reprobation. As David Engelsma, a present-day protégé of Hoeksema, puts it bluntly: a proper acknowledgment of God's electing of some persons to eternal life cannot be separated from the teaching "that God eternally hates some men; has immutably decreed their damnation; and has determined to withhold from them Christ, grace, faith, and salvation."[9] Any seeming good work performed by a reprobate, Engelsma argues, is in reality "foul with

9. David Engelsma, *Hyper-Calvinism and the Well-Meant Offer of the Gospel* (Grandville, MI: Reformed Free Publishing Association, 1994), 58.

depravity" in God's sight.[10] That is where I find myself taking another path.

To repeat, on the Hoeksema-Engelsma view, God simply hates the nonelect, along with all their thoughts and works. On this assessment, it would seem obvious that we as believers should also share in that hatred. The problem with taking that view, however, is that the Bible explicitly disallows it. Jesus himself reaffirms the second "great commandment," that we love our neighbor in the same way that we love our own selves (Mark 12:31). And he makes it clear that this love must even be extended to our enemies (Luke 6:27; Matt. 5:44).

In addressing this affirmation from our Lord himself, Hoeksema does not in any way back off from God's absolute hatred for the nonelect. "All the Scriptures," he says, "witness that God does not love, but hates His enemies and purposes to destroy them, except them He chose in Christ Jesus. . . . God does, indeed, love His [elect] enemies, but not as such, but as His children in Christ."[11] What does it mean, then, for the elect to love the *nonelect* enemies of God? Hoeksema warns us not to build too much empathy into the kind of love we are commanded to show toward unbelievers. The requisite "love is not a sentimental feeling or emotion or affection." The love we are to show toward the nonelect enemy of God "is not to flatter him, to have fellowship with him, to play games with him and to speak sweetly to him; but rather to rebuke him,

---

10. David Engelsma, *Common Grace Revisited: In Response to Richard J. Mouw's* He Shines in All That's Fair (Grandville, MI: Reformed Free Publishing Association, 2003), 41.

11. Herman Hoeksema, *The Protestant Reformed Churches in America: Their Origin, Early History, and Doctrine* (Grand Rapids: First Protestant Reformed Church, 1936), 317.

to demand that he leave his wicked way and thus to bless him and pray for him."[12]

David Engelsma typically follows the lead of his mentor Hoeksema, but in this case he does introduce an element of positive emotion into our love of the nonelect. Unlike the God we worship, Engelsma says, we Christians are "related to other humans by the strong ties of mutual flesh and blood." It is understandable, then, that feelings of human empathy will be stirred up toward those who do not share our faith. This is how God created us, and he does want us to love the neighbors with whom we share the bond of humanness. But God himself is not bound by that obligation to love. The reprobates are our neighbors, but not God's. God has no neighbors. While the Lord sees the nonelect as in reality "guilty, foul creatures," then, he commands us to have positive neighborly feelings toward persons whom he hates.[13]

Engelsma's softening, such as it is, of Hoeksema's formulation is significant. Hoeksema sets the tone for his confrontational depiction of the proper way to love the nonelect by describing our enemies as those who "despitefully use us, curse us and persecute us."[14] Christians have certainly experienced that kind of treatment throughout history. But that is hardly the whole story regarding our relations with non-Christian neighbors. Do we really want to discourage our children from playing with peers whom they meet at public playgrounds? Should we apply doctrinal tests when considering invitations to neighborhood gatherings?

Even as modified by Engelsma, then, the Protestant Reformed approach to the love of neighbor is seriously inadequate

---

12. Hoeksema, *Protestant Reformed Churches*, 318.
13. Engelsma, *Common Grace Revisited*, 45.
14. Hoeksema, *Protestant Reformed Churches*, 318.

as a basis for a biblically grounded ethic. Taken as a way of making an ontological claim, of course, there is nothing objectionable about saying that God himself has no neighbors.

> I am the LORD, and there is no other;
> apart from me there is no God. (Isa. 45:5)

But to use that reasonable claim about God's *totaliter aliter* being to restrict the range of divine love only to the elect is for many of us in the Calvinist tradition deeply unsatisfying. What do Hoeksema and Engelsma think is going on in the mind and heart of God in these matters? What could God have really been thinking and feeling when, on their interpretation, he commands believers to love their neighbors in the manner in which *he* loves *his* enemies? If the Lord sees each nonelect human being as thoroughly "guilty, foul creatures" whom he simply wants to "destroy," how does the word "love" even enter into a proper Calvinist ethic of neighbor relations?

A Typology of Divine Love

It may seem quite un-Calvinistic even to raise questions about what we might term "divine psychology." But this is exactly an area of theological focus that Benjamin Warfield probes at length in an essay, published in 1912, to which he gave the intriguing title "On the Emotional Life of Our Lord." Warfield makes it clear that we do not find out about God's love in the Bible simply by focusing on passages where the word "love" appears; in the Synoptic Gospels, for example, the actual word "love" appears only once. The emotion most frequently attributed to Jesus by the gospel writers is "compassion." But since compassion has love as its "foundation," Warfield argues, it is clear that "Jesus' prime characteristic was love."[15] Warfield points out that the one case in the Synoptics Gospels where love *is* explicitly attributed to Jesus is Jesus's encounter with the rich young ruler: "Jesus looked at him and loved him" (Mark 10:21). What is clearly implied in the account is that "our Savior turned yearningly to the rich young man and longed to do him good."[16] In his treatment of other specific cases, Warfield describes Jesus showing loving compassion to a variety of individuals and groups: blind persons, lepers, households, crowds milling about on city streets. Nor does Warfield show any interest in identifying which of these cases are salvific and which are not.

Engelsma and Hoeksema, on the other hand, would have to raise serious concerns about such cases. If, for example, the gospel account says that Jesus "loved" the rich young ruler, then surely this means, for them, that the young man was numbered among the elect. And one can see the Protestant Reformed theologians simply making that move. But things get somewhat more complicated in more "collective" instances of Jesus's compassion. What are we to make, from a soteriological perspective, of Jesus showing loving compassion for thousands of hungry people?

Around the same time that Warfield wrote his essay, his Princeton colleague Geerhardus Vos wrote an equally impressive essay, "The Scriptural Doctrine of the Love of God," where he pays explicit attention to the distinction between salvific and nonsalvific divine love. Like Warfield, Vos takes it for granted

15. Benjamin Breckinridge Warfield, "On the Emotional Life of Our Lord," in *Biblical and Theological Studies*, by the Members of the Faculty of Princeton Theological Seminary, published in commemoration of the 100th anniversary of the founding of the seminary (New York: Charles Scribner's Sons, 1912), 45.

16. Warfield, "On the Emotional Life," 45.

that God does manifest a form of love for the nonelect. Also like Warfield, he finds divine love on display in the pages of Scripture even when the word "love" is not used. Vos observes that while the Old Testament writers only infrequently make explicit references to "love"—the word finally shows up in the much-quoted Shema passage in Deuteronomy 6—the absence of "the direct use of the word by no means accurately measures the frequency and importance of the conception itself."[17] The Old Testament narrative, "in accordance with its Semitic genius, seldom views the divine attributes in the abstract as quiescent dispositions in God, but mostly as assuming concrete shape in their single historical manifestations."

What does loom large in the Old Testament, Vos observes, is the "special emphasis on the elective character of [divine] love." God made his covenant with Israel in particular (6), specifically in the context of "the sphere of the covenant." In Deuteronomy, for example, "the elective discriminating element in the origin of God's love for Israel is emphasized. He also did not choose many nations but gave His love to Israel alone" (8).

For all of that, though, this special emphasis on the particularized salvific love of God for Israel does not allow us to ignore, Vos argues, that the Old Testament acknowledges a divine love that reaches more widely than simply to the elect people. It is evident in the way that "God pledged to the whole of creation, in the day of Noah, [in] His abundant, ever-flowing kindness in the sphere of natural life, [in] His longsuffering in the view of universal sin, [and in] His common grace working for the restraint of sin" (18).

17. Geerhardus Vos, "The Scriptural Doctrine of the Love of God," *Presbyterian and Reformed Review*, no. 48 (January 1902): 6. Hereafter, page references from this work will be given in parentheses in the text.

This divine compassion, with its wide reach in the Old Testament witness, takes on a special focus in the New Testament writings, where we see in a graphic way the love of the Savior who, as Vos puts it, "was filled with tender compassion for every lost human soul, and was grieved even over those whose confirmed unbelief precluded all further hope of salvation." And since this compassion is so vividly depicted in the ministry of the incarnate Son, says Vos, "it is plain that there must be in God something corresponding to this" (22).

Vos directly challenges the kind of view developed by Hoeksema and Engelsma: "Love and wrath . . . are not mutually exclusive" in God, he says. God shows love to nonelect persons who, as unrepentant sinners, are also objects of his wrath. And while the elect have been mercifully delivered from the eternal consequences of the divine wrath against sin, they are also still subject, prior to their conscious acceptance of the claims of the gospel, "to the experience of the wrath of God" (35).

In allowing for nonsalvific displays of God's love, Vos does not see himself compromising his deep Calvinist convictions in any way, as is evident in his stern warning against blending God's complex dealing with human beings into an undifferentiated mix of divine love. To do so, he says, is to lose our focus on "the supreme soteriological manifestation of this love," which we see in the sovereign grace to that portion of the human race whom God has elected to eternal life (4).

3

Jacob, Esau . . . and Jesus

WE HAVE SEEN HOW WARFIELD and Vos want to preserve the mystery of God's purposes in electing individuals to eternal life while at the same time attending to God's nonsalvific favor toward all who are created in his image—and indeed toward the whole creation. Hoeksema and Engelsma, however, express quite a different spirit. They think this kind of expansive sense of God's love violates the basic tenets of Calvinist theology. What is going on in these differences?

In the past I have explained the differences by using the distinction the Japanese American theologian Kosuke Koyama made in an address to a gathering of theological educators in the 1990s. The Bible reveals God showing various moods throughout its complex narrative, Koyama observed: sometimes the Lord is angry, often he shows compassion, and there are times when, as the psalmist complains on occasion, God seems aloof.

It is important, Koyama said, that in our teaching we enable our theological students to see these various moods as expression of a coherent and consistent divine character. This means that each of us must decide whether the God we encounter on the pages of the Bible is "a generous God or a stingy God."

That comment generated an "Aha!" theological moment for me. When I heard Koyama say it, I was beginning to write in support of the theology of common grace against fellow Calvinists who rejected that perspective, and Koyama's observation made good sense of what I was experiencing. While I was drawn to the picture of God taking delight in some thoughts and deeds of non-Christians, other Calvinists clearly saw my view as heretical.

While I still find Koyama's observation helpful, I am not happy with the word "stingy" to characterize the Calvinists with whom I disagree. Theologians like Hoeksema and Engelsma do have a very profound sense of God's electing grace. They see the divine mercies at work in the salvation of sinners as generous beyond our human capacity to conceive. My disagreement with them is not about the wonders of divine generosity as such, but about the range of human beings to which God extends various manifestations of generosity.

Koyama talked about *deciding* what kind of God we are going to encounter in the Bible. This cannot however mean that we decide ahead of time what we want the Bible to say and then focus on things that reinforce our preferences. That is not a healthy theological approach. Whatever expectations that we bring to our reading of the Bible have to be shaped and reshaped by what the Word itself says. We need to stay open to new insights, new considerations, new anticipations regarding what we encounter on the pages of Scripture.

I don't doubt that Calvinists who see things differently from what I see are doing all of that. Yet they read the patterns of God's dealings with human beings differently than I do. Why?

The Role of "Stance"

Gijsbert van den Brink's book exploring the often complex issues in the relationship between religious faith and scientific pursuits has helped me clarify all this. In explaining that he is writing from an orthodox Reformed theological perspective, van den Brink observes that to be Reformed is not so much to embrace a closed system of theology as it is to adopt "a specific stance—that is, an intensification of some theological doctrines, commitments and even debates (e.g., on free will) that can also be found, but less emphatically, in other parts of the universal church."[1] What makes a theological perspective Reformed is that it addresses theological issues with a certain "accent" that also expresses itself in unique "intensifications of catholic affirmations."[2]

I like the way van den Brink links the idea of theological "stance" with "accents" and "intensifications." It comports nicely with my own understanding of what it means to be a Calvinist. Our Reformed affirmation of the sovereignty of God is something we share with Thomas Aquinas, Martin Luther, and John Wesley. And we also share with them an acknowledgment of the reality of human responsibility. But we Calvinists adopt a unique "stance" toward those teachings, such that if anyone suggests that human freedom in some way restricts the divine rule over all things, we will quickly come to the defense of the full sovereignty of God.

Lutherans certainly affirm the sovereignty of God, but not with the same emphasis that we Calvinists put on that teaching.

---

1. Gijsbert van den Brink, *Reformed Theology and Evolutionary Theory* (Grand Rapids: Eerdmans, 2020), 63–64.
2. Van den Brink, *Reformed Theology*, 67.

They, in turn, "intensify" the doctrine of justification by faith, which leads to their speaking with different "accents" than our Calvinist discussions of the subject. The Wesleyan "stance" regarding the centrality of "holiness" produces yet another theological pattern, with its own unique "accents."

But van den Brink's "stance" notion can also apply *within* confessional camps. A personal example. I was raised in the conservative strand within the Reformed Church in America (RCA). When I joined the Calvin College faculty in my late twenties, I became a member of the Christian Reformed Church (CRC). While the two Dutch-background denominations share a general stance and, with their shared confessional standards, can talk to each other with a similar theological accent, the CRC's theological "intensifications" differed, sometimes in subtle ways and in other ways not so subtle, from the RCA's. The CRC had experienced different debates in its past than the RCA had, which produced different "intensifications."

How do we assess the theological adequacy of a "stance"? Here I am convinced that a little bit of relativism is permissible, even required. What a group gets "intense" about in its theology has something to do not only with its historical experiences, but also with matters of temperament, with aesthetic sensitivities, and with features embedded in its cultural context. The recognition that these factors are at work, however, should not keep us from also addressing important issues of truth. Fidelity to what God has revealed in Scripture is of crucial importance.

Serving the Common Good

In one of my published discussions of common grace, I mentioned, pretty much in passing, that I have on occasion wondered what it would be like if Herman Hoeksema served as mayor of Grand Rapids.[3] He would have been required to seek the welfare of people whom he firmly believed that God has hated from all eternity.

Strictly speaking, of course, Hoeksema could have come up with (getting some needed help from Engelsma!) a theological basis for the mayoral task. The God who hates the non-Christian portion of the city's citizenry commands us to love them, since we have a human bond with these folks that God—who has no neighbors—does not share. A Hoeksema-type Calvinist has divine permission, then, to act on feelings of empathy for needy human beings.

Hoeksema might come up with a theological rationale of this sort for serving as mayor, but one wonders how consistently he could sustain a good will toward those citizens he sees as objects of unmixed divine hatred. The theological basis in Hoeksema's theology is certainly less robust—less "intense"!—than what is emphasized in the long tradition in Calvinism that has seen political service—seeking the common good—as a positive Christian calling. Abraham Kuyper, for one, found a strong theological basis for his service in the Dutch parliament, as did Herman Bavinck.[4] And John Calvin himself was actively engaged in public policy matters in Geneva.[5]

---

3. Richard J. Mouw, *All That God Cares About: Common Grace and Divine Delight* (Grand Rapids: Brazos, 2020), 54.

4. Two excellent biographies of each of these neo-Calvinist pioneers give detailed attention to the development of their political thought and their public engagements: James Bratt, *Abraham Kuyper: Modern Calvinist, Christian Democrat* (Grand Rapids: Eerdmans, 2013), and James Eglinton, *Herman Bavinck: A Critical Biography* (Grand Rapids: Baker Academic, 2020).

5. W. Fred Graham, *The Constructive Revolutionary: John Calvin and His Socio-Economic Impact* (Richmond, VA: John Knox, 1971).

To raise this concern is to point to a relevant factor in evaluating "stances." To what degree does one's theology—with its "intensifications" and "accents"—provide encouragement, guidance, and motivation for a legitimate area of kingdom service?

Narrative Coherence

One key criterion for assessing the merits of theological "stances" has to do with the way in which our "intensifications" of specific themes and passages do justice to the overall biblical narrative. Does our interpretation of one biblical passage comport in reasonable ways with other relevant biblical data?

I struggle with my own "stance" on a biblical passage that has been much "intensified" in our Calvinist tradition: Paul's use of the Jacob and Esau story in Romans 9. Even before the twin boys were born, the apostle says, with neither of them having yet "done anything good or bad," God had ordained the following (here Paul quotes Malachi 1:2–3): "Jacob I loved, but Esau I hated" (vv. 11–13). Thus, God has mercy on whom he wants to have mercy, and he hardens whom he wants to harden (v. 15).

Over the years I have wrestled with different interpretations of this passage proposed by Calvinist scholars, and I still have not made up my mind how exactly it fits into my overall theological perspective. I do see this Romans 9 passage as revealed truth, though, and I accept it in the manner nicely captured by Geerhardus Vos. The teaching here, Vos says, is shrouded in mystery, for which God has his own "wise and holy reasons." But this mystery does not "allow us to assert that election and preterition are arbitrary decrees to the mind of God." We must simply accept the divine motives as "inscrutable to us."[6] I am content to live with that kind of recognition of divine inscrutability, without trying to say more on the subject. I certainly have problems with Engelsma's insistence, mentioned earlier, that God's hatred of Esau is a pure and eternal hatred—which means that there can never be any instance when God approves something Esau says or does.

To pursue the argument with Engelsma and Hoeksema on this particular point would require complex explorations of metaphysical issues. But for me the issue comes down to a concern for the coherence of the overall biblical narrative about Jacob and Esau in particular. Genesis 33 offers a dramatic account of the reunion of the twin brothers, after a long period of separation occasioned by Jacob's deceiving his father into giving him a blessing that belonged by birthright to Esau. When Esau had learned about what happened, he vowed to kill Jacob, who then fled to live among his mother's kinfolk, where he married and prospered.

There came a time, though, when the Lord commanded Jacob to return to his home territory, and he obeyed, even though he feared the wrath of Esau. Much to his surprise and relief, however, when he finally approached his brother, bowing in a spirit of penitence, Esau warmly embraced him and the two brothers wept together.

The Sunday school version of that story that I was taught as a child depicted this as a touching scene, in which Esau is seen in a highly favorable light for the wonderfully forgiving spirit that he showed to Jacob. We children were given the clear impression that God looked upon that scene of brotherly reconciliation with approval.

6. Geerhardus Vos, "The Scriptural Doctrine of the Love of God," *Presbyterian and Reformed Review*, no. 48 (January 1902): 23.

The Protestant Reformed theological perspective obviously raises doubts about that portrayal, however. If God hates Esau with an eternal hatred, then what might seem like a laudable act of forgiveness on Esau's part is something that in God's eyes is "foul with depravity." Also, how does God assess *Jacob's* role in this encounter? Is God happy that Jacob accepted his brother's forgiving embrace? On the kind of softened reading that Engelsma might give, it would seem that the Lord was pleased, since God created the two brothers as human beings with strong familial ties. Jacob has the obligation to love his brother as he loves himself, and it is with deep and humble gratitude that he accepts his brother's embrace, since he knows that he has sinned against his brother. So God looks down on a scene where someone he eternally loves responds with brotherly—neighborly—affection to someone God eternally hates. That is obviously not how Warfield and Vos would encourage us to see the encounter, however. They would approve of my Sunday school teacher's version of the story.

A Trinitarian Love

We can take the question of how God saw the reconciliation of Jacob and Esau a step further. Suppose Jesus had encountered such a scene during his earthly ministry. It seems obvious from the surveys offered by Warfield and Vos that the Savior would have looked upon their embrace with empathy—and not just in his human nature, but in his divinity. It would be interesting to find out how Hoeksema and Engelsma would read that situation.

Much is at stake in how we answer this question. There is no good theological basis for positing an attitudinal gap between the God of the Old Testament and the Savior of the Gospels. Jesus who as the Word become flesh is the same God who chose Israel from among the nations to be his redeemed people. And that sovereign deity who elected Israel by grace alone is the same God who, in Abraham Kuyper's memorable words describing the ministry of the incarnate Son, "does not hold back His hand from the touch of leprous flesh."[7]

It is theologically necessary to remind ourselves that the electing God about whom Paul writes in Romans 9 is the *triune* God. We cannot separate what we are told in that passage from what we also learn by attending to the ministry of Jesus as he walked the paths of Palestine. Nor can we, in understanding the character and extent of divine love, ignore the work of the Holy Spirit, as we will see when we look in detail at how Warfield and several of his orthodox Calvinist contemporaries made the case for the Spirit as the divine agent of salvific generosity.

7. Abraham Kuyper, *Christianity and the Class Struggle*, trans. Dirk Jellema (Grand Rapids: Piet Heyn, 1950), 27–28.

4

Those Not "Outwardly Called"

DARRYL HART AND I SHARE a high regard for the "Old Princeton" theologians, particularly the ones I have already mentioned: Charles Hodge, A. A. Hodge, Benjamin Breckinridge Warfield, and Geerhardus Vos. Those thinkers, each with a well-deserved reputation for a commitment to traditional Calvinism, held sway at Princeton Theological Seminary from the mid-nineteenth century into the 1920s.

However, Hart and I have quite different reasons for appreciating their theological influence. In the title of his essay discussing their collective contributions, Hart commends them for their "unoriginal Calvinism." He says they contributed very few new ideas. Rather, for them, "repeating the truths of the Calvinist wing of the Protestant Reformation, no matter how boring or predictable, was a matter of pride."[1] Given the widespread heterodoxies that characterized so much of nineteenth-century North American theology, their "unoriginality turned out to

1. D. G. Hart, "Systematic Theology at Old Princeton Seminary: Unoriginal Calvinism," in *The Pattern of Sound Doctrine: Systematic Theology at the Westminster Seminaries*, ed. David VanDrunen (Phillipsburg, NJ: P&R, 2004), 3–4.

be remarkably adept at preserving the content and character of Reformed orthodoxy."[2]

In disagreeing with Hart's assessment, I offer the essays, discussed earlier, by Warfield and Vos as evidence. I do not find those essays either "boring or predictable." Each of them is a gift of theological lucidity that challenges many stereotypes of Calvinist thought—and in a manner that speaks profoundly to some present-day theological concerns.

In this chapter I will detail what I see as further evidence of their originality, a contribution that seldom gets any serious attention in recent writings evaluating their work. During the final few decades of the nineteenth century, serious debates took place among Presbyterians in the United States about the need for significant revisions to the Westminster Confession. Those who actively promoted confessional revisionism wanted to eliminate Westminster's reference to the pope as the antichrist, as well as advocating for a clarification on the "free offer" of the gospel. The theological item that most exercised the traditionalists, though, had do with the salvific status of children who die in infancy.

The Princeton theologians were not opposed to confessional revision as such. But they were troubled by the perceived motives of those insisting on revision. The active revisionists were convinced that the Westminster Confession depicted a rather harsh God who intentionally distributed his salvific blessings in limited ways, and they wanted the Confession to portray a more expansive range of the divine mercies. Warfield and his allies read the theology of Westminster differently; they were convinced of the importance of interpreting the Confession in a way that made some of the proposed revisions unnecessary.

2. Hart, "Systematic Theology," 26.

They also labeled the revisionists' depiction of divine harshness in the Confession as a misreading of the theological intentions of the Westminster Assembly. But the orthodox were open to revision on one specific article in the Confession.

That article had to do with the salvific status of dying infants, as treated in the third section of the Confession's tenth chapter, "Of Effectual Calling": "Elect infants, dying in infancy, are regenerated and saved by Christ through the Spirit, who worketh when, and where, and how he pleaseth. So also are all other elect persons who are incapable of being outwardly called by the ministry of the Word."[3]

The Princeton Calvinists were convinced that this declaration had to be understood in less harsh terms than were often alleged by their more liberal opponents—and even by some of their fellow conservatives. They were joined in this conviction by a fellow traditionalist, W. G. T. Shedd, a faculty member at New York's Union Theological Seminary. Shedd's overall theological perspective was the same as those of his friends at Princeton.

In this denominational debate, the Princeton theologians agreed with those pushing for a confessional revision that makes it clear that God saves *all* children who die before they are capable of understanding the claims of the gospel. So, while they worked for that change, they clearly were not ready to support many additional revisions. As Shedd argued in his 1893 book defending the theology of the Westminster Confession, doctrinal revision should be "a rare occurrence in ecclesiastical history." Those who propose changes, he said, are typically "in favor of

3. Westminster Confession of Faith, chap. 10, sec. 3, in *The Creeds of Christendom, with a History and Critical Notes,* ed. Philip Schaff, vol. 3 (Grand Rapids: Baker Books, 1996), 625.

vague and looser statements." The doctrinal drift that was so evident in the broad Christian community meant, for Shedd, that it was "of the utmost importance that the regenerate Church, in all its denominations, should stand firm in the old paths."[4] Warfield argued along similar lines. While he would not insist that the Reformation-era confessions should never be revised, he feared that as a result of the current revisionist efforts, "these time-honored formularies" would be "patched up with scraps of cruder new thinking."[5]

The revisionist campaign culminated in 1903, and the results were not the worst-case scenario feared by the orthodox. The General Assembly eliminated the reference to the pope as the antichrist and added two chapters to the Confession, one on the Holy Spirit and the other on missions and the free offer; and they issued supplementary clarifications on the divine decrees.

Most important, though, was the decision not to alter the wording of the third section of the Confession's tenth chapter, "Of Effectual Calling." The assembly simply issued a "Declaratory Statement" approving the expansive interpretation for which the orthodox party had argued, namely, "that *all* dying in infancy are included in the election of grace, and are regenerated and saved by Christ through the Spirit."[6]

Again, both sides agreed on the theological point being made in that clarifying statement. What they had been dis-

4. William G. T. Shedd, *Calvinism Pure and Mixed: A Defence of the Westminster Standards* (Carlisle, PA: Banner of Truth Trust, 1986), 10–11.

5. Benjamin Warfield, *On the Revision of the Confession of Faith* (New York: Anson D. F. Randolph and Co., 1890), 15, 17. This publication consists of five polemical pieces Warfield wrote for Presbyterian magazines during 1889–1890. The booklet is accessible at: https://en.wikisource.org/wiki/On_the_Revision_of_the_Confession_of_Faith.

6. Declaratory Statement (1903) of the Presbyterian Church in the United States of America, in Schaff, *The Creeds of Christendom*, 3:920–21.

puting was whether the theological point expressed the actual intentions of the original drafters of the Confession. The revisionists were convinced that the wording of the Confession was intended to allow for the view that the dying infants of non-Christian parents were damned, while Shedd and Warfield insisted that the Confession was not drafted from that kind of "harsh God" perspective.

During the decade prior to the 1903 Declaratory Statement, Shedd had argued that the Westminster article's reference to "elect infants, dying" was meant not as a contrast to *non*elect dying infants but rather to "elect infants not dying in infancy." This way of seeing it, he observed, means that "there are no non-elect dying infants"; all children who die in infancy are saved.[7] Along the same lines, Warfield contended that the contrast that the Westminster divines had in mind was "between 'elect infants that reach the adult state,' who are saved by the 'word and Spirit,' and 'elect infants dying in infancy' who are saved by the Spirit apart from the word."[8] And, he confessed, "for myself, I believe with all my heart that all dying in infancy are saved, and I believe that I can prove it from Scripture."[9]

Neither Warfield nor Shedd denied that Calvinists in the past had taught infant damnation. But, Shedd argued, that view could actually serve as a basis for a "widening of the circle of infant election."[10] Shedd used Augustine as a case in point. Augustine's contention that some dying infants are damned was linked to his refusal to weaken the doctrine of original sin. All human beings under fallen conditions are born with "a cor-

---

7. Shedd, *Calvinism Pure and Mixed*, 113.
8. Warfield, *On the Revision*, 52.
9. Warfield, *On the Revision*, 55.
10. Shedd, *Calvinism Pure and Mixed*, 109.

rupt disposition" and are thus deserving of eternal death.[11] Augustine was right, said Shedd, to refuse any minimizing of the punishment due to our sinful nature. What Augustine failed to see, though, is that if "the infinite compassion of God frees all [dying infants] from the dreadful guilt and penalty by the blood of atonement," then explicitly stating this view would actually "have magnified the divine mercy."[12] And this magnification, Shedd insisted, finds its expression in the Westminster Confession.

We see from Shedd's comments on Augustine that he and Warfield were adamant that their inclusive understanding of "elect infants" not be understood as in any way undercutting the Calvinist insistence on the doctrine of total depravity. Warfield and Shedd did not want to create a special category for children as such. When salvation is extended to adults or to very young children, it is always a gift of sovereign grace to individual guilty sinners who are worthy of damnation.

The Intentions of Westminster

The insistence by the orthodox Calvinists that Westminster did not allow for infant damnation came under sharp attack, most notably by the prominent church historian Philip Schaff. The Confession's use of the term "*elect* infants," Schaff argued, clearly implied a contrast to infants who are "nonelect." Not only is the Warfield-Shedd interpretation of the article in question "ungrammatical and illogical,"[13] but it is clearly contradicted, Schaff

---

11. Shedd, *Calvinism Pure and Mixed*, 107.

12. Shedd, *Calvinism Pure and Mixed*, 109–10.

13. Philip Schaff, *Creed Revision in the Presbyterian Churches* (New York: Charles Scribner's Sons, 1890), 17.

contended, by the expressed views regarding the damnation of infants from key members of the Westminster Assembly—an assessment that Schaff supported with several citations.[14] Denial of the reality of the influence of damnation-of-infants teachings at Westminster has to be seen as "irreconcilable with the theology and terminology of the Confession, and this departure should be frankly acknowledged."[15] For all of that, though, Schaff did acknowledge that, even if the traditionalists' support for the "all infants" understanding was based on faulty historical grounds, their theological views on the subject were "a progress in the right direction."[16]

In 1900, J. V. Stephens published a book-length overview of the Northern Presbyterian debate about the "elect infants" topic, and he was less kind toward the traditionalists than Schaff. Stephens was a theologian in the Cumberland Presbyterian movement, a group that had officially departed from strict Calvinism in favor of some key Arminian teachings. He expanded on some of Schaff's historical data to insist that the Westminster Assembly had been *dominated* by advocates of infant damnation. Thus, while Shedd and the Princeton theologians had arrived at the right perspective in their "all infants" view, their allegations regarding the intentions of the drafters of the Confession were not to be trusted. They were failing to acknowledge, Stephens argued, that by the nineteenth century the harsh views of members of the Assembly had come to be replaced among Presbyterians by the more inclusivist understanding. Thus, the orthodox Calvinists were now simply using faulty historical claims to disguise their own willingness to

14. Schaff, *Creed Revision*, 19.
15. Schaff, *Creed Revision*, 20.
16. Schaff, *Creed Revision*, 20.

read a "modern interpretation" back into the deliberations of the Westminster Assembly.[17]

The historical case made by Schaff and Stephens has plausibility. The orthodox party could have been wrong about what the Westminster divines actually had in mind when they approved the phrase "elect infants, dying in infancy." But they could also have gotten *something* right, at least in the sense that the Westminster divines intentionally *allowed for* an "all infants" understanding in what they declared. Schaff himself acknowledges the possibility that the drafters of this article in the Confession purposely allowed for differing interpretations: "The Confession nowhere speaks of reprobate infants, and the existence of such is not *necessarily* implied by way of distinction, although it *probably* was in the minds of the framers as their private opinion, which they wisely withheld from the Confession."[18]

Regenerating Acts

We can leave things where Schaff does on this. The important point is that the orthodox Calvinists gave their theological support to the view that all dying infants are saved. What is even more significant for my purposes here is that these theologians also addressed a broader issue in the Westminster article in which the "elect infants" reference appears. That same section 10 in article 10 goes on to affirm that "the Spirit . . . worketh when,

---

17. J. V. Stephens, *Elect Infants; or, Infant Salvation in the Westminster Symbols* (Victoria, Australia: Leopold Classic Library, 2016), 175–76.

18. Philip Schaff, *The History of Creeds*, in *The Creeds of Christendom, with a History and Critical Notes*, ed. Philip Schaff, vol. 1 (Grand Rapids: Baker Books, 1996), 795.

and where, and how he pleaseth," including in the lives of "all other elect persons who are incapable of being outwardly called by the ministry of the Word."

At first glance it may seem odd that the Confession would make a point of explicitly linking the salvation of children dying in infancy to an additional category of "all other elect persons" who also have no access to the proclamation of the gospel. There are, however, some uniquely Reformed theological issues at stake here. In stipulating that the Spirit on occasion regenerates individuals apart from the proclamation of the Word, the divines thought it important to emphasize that children, like all sinful adults, can only be saved by a gracious regenerating act of the Holy Spirit.

We can illustrate the point here by looking at the difference between the Reformed view and that of some Calvinists in the Baptist tradition. In an essay entitled "Why We Believe Children Who Die Go to Heaven," Southern Baptist theologians Albert Mohler and Daniel Akin argue that while all human beings, whether young or older, "are guilty of original sin," there is nonetheless a biblically based "distinction between original sin and actual sins," since "moral responsibility and understanding is necessary for actual sins." And because children have not yet committed actual sins for which they are accountable, God does not see them in the same light as adults who know what is right and yet fail to do it. In judging human beings, God takes into account the difference between an adult who "knows to do right and does not do it" and a child who is "incapable of such decisions."[19]

19. R. Albert Mohler Jr. and Daniel L. Akin, "Why We Believe Children Who Die Go to Heaven," Pickens First Baptist, January 25, 2017, https://www.fbcpickens.org/why-we-believe-children-who-die-go-to-heaven/.

At first glance, it may appear that the view of these Baptist theologians is not that far removed from that of the Reformed Calvinists. What is significant, though, is that Mohler and Akin are making a case for children in general, whereas Shedd and his Princeton friends are staying with Westminster's specific focus on children "dying in infancy." They are not positing a special category for children as such. All human beings, including dying infants, are deserving of eternal punishment and can only be saved by individual acts of divine grace. Shedd puts that point clearly: "Though the infant has committed no acts of known and wilful transgression, yet his heart is estranged from God, and his will is at enmity with the holy law of God. . . . An infant, therefore, needs salvation because he is really culpable and punishable. He requires the whole work of the Redeemer, both as expiating guilt and cleansing from pollution."[20] The Westminster article on "elect infants" underscores this instance by stating explicitly that dying infants are saved in the same manner as the subgroup of *adults* who are regenerated by the Spirit apart from the proclamation of the Word. Both infants and adults are condemned by God for their fallen natures and are worthy of eternal punishment for their sinfulness. If any individual—infant or adult—is saved, it must be by a bestowal on that individual of sovereign grace alone.

At the risk of belaboring this point, we can also see a clear contrast between the view of Reformed Calvinism and Catholic teachings regarding the salvation of persons who have no access to the Christian message. In the Vatican II document *Lumen Gentium*, the gathered bishops described persons "who, through no fault of their own, do not know the Gospel of Christ or his Church, but who nevertheless seek God with a sincere heart,

20. Shedd, *Calvinism Pure and Mixed*, 107.

and, moved by grace, try in their actions to do his will as they know it through the dictates of their conscience."[21]

While Reformed theologians have also typically acknowledged a continuing role of conscience in fallen humanity, for them conscientious "dictates" play a somewhat different kind of role. The Canons of Dort, for example, acknowledge that "glimmerings of natural light" can be seen in the unredeemed human consciousness, but the Canons immediately warn us against seeing these "glimmerings" as having any sort of salvific value. This is typical of the Reformation-era Reformed confessional statements about the noetic remnants of our unfallen condition. The Westminster Confession, for example, says that what we know about God and his purposes apart from special revelation has no salvific merit, but simply serves to "leave men inexcusable,"[22] and similarly, the Belgic Confession says that such knowledge in the unredeemed serves mainly to "leave them without excuse."[23]

Shedd's argument follows along these confessional lines. Human conscience on its own, he says, plays no role in motivating the unredeemed to do the will of God. But the Spirit does make use of the remnants of conscience to bring an elect sinner to salvation, by bringing about a sorrow for sin along with a realization of being totally dependent on a forgiving mercy that must come outside of any resource that the sinner can find

21. Dogmatic Constitution on the Church, *Lumen Gentium*, Solemnly Promulgated by His Holiness, Pope Paul VI, on November 21, 1964, chap. 2, section 16, accessible at http://www.vatican.va/archive/hist_councils/ii_vat ican_council/documents/vat-ii_const_19641121_lumen-gentium_en.html, accessed 4/24/2020.

22. Westminster Confession of Faith, chap. 1, sec. 1, in Schaff, *The Creeds of Christendom*, 3:600.

23. Belgic Confession, article 2, in Schaff, *The Creeds of Christendom*, 1:384.

within.[24] And Shedd, in line with the Westminster article's reference to "all others," sees this work of the Holy Spirit operating in the lives of some adult persons who do not have access to the proclamation of the Word.

While Shedd went further than some of his Princeton friends in pursuing the details regarding this operation of the Spirit, they did share his explicit endorsement of Westminster's reference to "other elect persons" who are regenerated by the Spirit apart from the Word. A. A. Hodge, for one, set forth the same general themes that guided Shedd's explorations on the subject. Already in 1869, before the revisionist controversy heated up, Hodge had pointed out that the Westminster article on "elect infants" also allowed that there are adult individuals who are directly "regenerated and sanctified immediately by God *without the use of means.*"[25] And then shortly before his death in 1886, he reaffirmed his approval of what the Westminster article sets forth. Through the atoning work of Christ, he wrote, "not only all adult believers, but all dying in infancy, all idiots [*sic*] and all who have been saved by any extraordinary means known only to God, are reconciled to God and stand absolved from guilt."[26]

Warfield showed some reluctance to say as much as Shedd or A. A. Hodge did on "other elect persons." Indeed, in a booklet he published in 1918 entitled *Are They Few That Be Saved?*[27] he explicitly distanced himself from how Shedd

24. Shedd, *Calvinism Pure and Mixed*, 128–29.

25. A. A. Hodge, *The Confession of Faith* (Carlisle, PA: Banner of Truth Trust, 1958), 174–75 (emphasis added).

26. A. A. Hodge, *Evangelical Theology: Lectures on Doctrine* (Carlisle, PA: Banner of Truth Trust, 1976), 218.

27. Benjamin Warfield, *Are They Few That Be Saved?* (New York: Our Hope Publications, 1918), n. 39. The online version of this booklet that has

saw the implications of the "other elect persons" reference. At the same time, though, Warfield developed his own case for the view that "the immensely greater part of the human race" will be saved in the end, and then included Shedd in the list of the "honored names" of recent Calvinist "prophets of our own."[28]

While the nineteenth-century Calvinist "prophets" whom Warfield had in mind certainly disagreed regarding some theological specifics, they clearly shared a common desire to advocate for a Calvinism guided by a spirit of salvific generosity. The debate over elect infants provided the occasion to demonstrate that this spirit of generosity was perfectly compatible with a nonnegotiable commitment to sovereign electing grace as the only hope for human beings who are otherwise lost in their depraved condition.

We need to be clear, however, that these orthodox theologians were not simply accommodating their Calvinism to modern "nonjudgmental" sentiments in religious matters, as Stephens had alleged. Nor were they just repeating typical Calvinist teachings of the past. They were working together to promote a celebration of divine generosity that they found in the Westminster Confession itself, and they committed themselves to correcting what they saw as widespread misunderstandings of the spirit of the Calvinism as embodied in that Confession.

---

footnotes is unpaginated: https://reformed.org/eschaton/few_saved.pdf, accessed April 24, 2020; the footnote here is found on the final page. From here on I will refer to the paginated version of the "epub" copy at https://www.monergism.com/are-they-few-be-saved-ebook.

28. Warfield, *Are They Few?*, 23.

Mere "Unoriginality"?

This brings me back to my disagreement with Darryl Hart. Is it really fair to say, as Hart does, that the genius of the Old Princeton theologians' contributions to nineteenth-century Presbyterianism—in an alliance with their fellow Calvinist Shedd—was expressed in their willingness to be "boring" and "predictable" in their dedication to "unoriginality"? Is it fair to describe these orthodox theologians as simply content to repeat what Calvinists of the past had said?

I think not. On the most cynical reading of their motives, they were deliberately passing off what Stephens labeled a "modern interpretation" as if it were the view held by the drafters of the Westminster Confession. Or, on Schaff's more charitable characterization, they were on the side of those who wanted to foster theological "progress" by advocating for a less harsh Calvinism than previous expressions.

And the new ways essentially meant arguing forcefully for a generous understanding of the teaching that, while God's saving purposes are normally accomplished by the Spirit working in coordination with the preaching of the Word, God is willing to dispense his sovereign mercies in situations where the Word is not effectively proclaimed. Warfield and his colleagues wanted a declaration of salvific generosity that was fully on display in Jesus—the One who, when he returned to his heavenly Throne, sent into the world a Spirit "who worketh when, and where, and how he pleaseth."

5

More Than a "Remnant"

IN 2004 I PUBLISHED A SHORT BOOK (144 pages) with the title *Calvinism in the Las Vegas Airport*. It wasn't a technical theological treatise. I took my point of departure from a scene in a film, *Hard Core*, directed by Calvin College alumnus Paul Schrader, who went on to receive acclaim in Hollywood for his films, where a stern Dutch Reformed elder, played by George C. Scott, tried to explain the theology of the Canons of Dort to a neopagan teenager in the Las Vegas airport. My basic point was that the effort would have been more effective if the elder had introduced her to Calvinism with the first question and answer of the Heidelberg Catechism, the warm Calvinist confession that "my only comfort in life and in death" is to "belong to my faithful Savior Jesus Christ."[1]

While my book was generally well received, one of the twelve chapters, chapter 8, drew some serious theological criticism. Those critical concerns did not come as a surprise.

---

1. Heidelberg Catechism, Question and Answer 1, in *The Creeds of Christendom, with a History and Critical Notes*, ed. Philip Schaff, vol. 3 (Grand Rapids: Baker Books, 1996), 307–8.

A reader of the prepublication version of the manuscript told me there would be some trouble with what I said. After positive comments about the rest of the book, he wrote to me about this chapter: "Rich, this one makes me nervous!"

I want here to go back to what I said in that chapter,[2] covering the same territory but in more detail. My purpose is to get a better understanding of the topic that has traditionally been referred to as "the number of the elect."

When I started to write that chapter, I wanted to rely on the views of the solid Calvinist theologians whom I most admired, on the number of the elect. My own impulse was to argue for a large total, but I fully expected that my theological heroes would convince me otherwise on the basis of their biblical expositions. What I found in reading several of the Old Princeton theologians, however, was an even more expansive view than I had been nurturing. Here, for example, is a comment that surprised me by Charles Hodge's son Archibald, about his father's thoughts on the subject:

> My father at the close of his long life spent in the defense of Calvinism, wrote on one of his conference papers, in trembling characters, a little while before he died, "I am fully persuaded that the vast majority of the human race will share in the beatitudes and glories of our Lord's redemption." Remember that all who die before complete moral agency have been given to Christ. Remember that the vast populations of the coming millenniums are given to Christ. Then shall the promises of Christ to the great Father of the faithful

2. Chapter 8, "The Generosity Option," in Richard J. Mouw, *Calvinism in the Las Vegas Airport: Making Connections in Today's World* (Grand Rapids: Zondervan, 2004), 83–91.

be fulfilled to the letter: "Thy seed shall be like the sands of the sea-shore;" "Thy seed shall be like the stars of heaven for multitude," and recollect that when God made this promise, while Abraham saw only with the naked eye, God took in far more than even the telescopic heavens in magnitude.[3]

In looking further into the elder Hodge's theology, I discovered that what he had written in those "trembling characters" was actually a summary of what he had articulated at greater length when at the height of his scholarly powers. Here, for example, is a quote from the penultimate paragraph of his *Systematic Theology*: "We have reason to believe ... that the number of the finally lost in comparison with the whole number of the saved will be very inconsiderable. Our blessed Lord, when surrounded by the innumerable company of the redeemed, will be hailed as the 'Salvator Hominum,' the Savior of Men, as the Lamb that bore the sins of the world."[4]

I had not expected to find this "large number" perspective in the Hodges, and I was surprised to find it also being advocated for by other nineteenth-century Calvinist stalwarts. The obvious question this raised in my mind was how they reconciled their salvific optimism with those biblical passages that emphasized a small number of the elect.

My questions were addressed at length by Benjamin Warfield, in his essay *Are They Few That Be Saved?*, where he argues against the *paucitas salvandorum*, Latin for the view that only a small remnant will be saved in the end. While opposing this perspective, he treats it with considerable respect, giving careful attention to

3. A. A. Hodge, *Evangelical Theology: Lectures on Doctrine* (Edinburgh: Banner of Truth Trust, 1976), 401.

4. Charles Hodge, *Systematic Theology*, vol. 3 (Peabody, MA: Hendrickson, 2003), 879–80.

the writing of his friend Abraham Kuyper, whose advocacy for a small-number perspective provides a "striking illustration"[5] of the firm grip that the doctrine has had on so many in the Calvinist tradition. Warfield sees some irony in Kuyper's views on this subject since, he observes, Kuyper affirms so many admirable things that would seem to stand in tension with the small-number view, especially "the great fact on which he has repeatedly and very fruitfully insisted, that it is 'mankind as an organic whole which is saved' and the lost are accordingly only individuals who have been cut off from the stem of humanity" (6).[6]

Warfield shows how Kuyper illustrates this organic emphasis by introducing the image of humankind as a tree that "has grown up out of Adam." We can think of the ground beneath strewn with leaves and small branches that have fallen off. Warfield points out that for Kuyper, "the lost are the branches, twigs and leaves which have fallen away from the stem of mankind, while the elect alone remain attached to it. Not the stem itself goes to destruction, leaving only a few golden leaflets strewn on the fields of eternal light, but, on the contrary, the stem, the tree, the race abides, and what is lost is broken from the stem and loses its organic connection" (6–7). Warfield clearly sees Kuyper's eloquent use of these expansive images here as grounds for rejecting the small-number view. The surprise for Warfield is that Kuyper

> conceives himself bound to explain that the tree of humanity which abides may be, and in point of fact is, less in actual mass than the branches which are broken off for the burning.

5. Benjamin Warfield, *Are They Few That Be Saved?* (New York: Our Hope Publications, 1918), 5. Hereafter, page references from this work will be given in parentheses in the text.

6. Warfield is quoting here from what are apparently his own translations of writings by Kuyper in Dutch.

It is of the very nature of an organic as distinguished from a mechanical object, he argues, that it can suffer changes— even such as contract and curtail it—without losing its identity. "The human race," he explains, "is thus to be compared to a tree which has been pruned and now again shoots up in a smaller size. The ruin of the genus humanum is not restored in its entirety; it becomes in its reconstitution an organism of smaller proportions. The Church, thus, conceived as the reconstitution of the human race, forms an organism of smaller compass, . . . a little flock. . . . 'For many are called, but few chosen,' Mat. 7;14, Lk. 13;23." (7)

Warfield looks at length at the biblical verses that Kuyper and others appeal to in defending the small-number view, and interacts in detail with the exegetical and theological treatments of a number of scholars. Here is Warfield's summary of his reading of the key biblical texts:

A scrutiny of these passages will make it sufficiently apparent that they do not form an adequate basis for the tremendous conclusion which has been founded on them. In all of them alike our Lord's purpose is rather ethical impression than prophetic disclosure. Spoken out of the immediate circumstances of the time to the immediate needs of those about Him, His words supply valid motives to action to all who find themselves with similar needs in like circumstances; but they cannot be read as assurances that the circumstances intimated or implied are necessarily constant and must remain forever unchanged. What He says is directed to inciting His hearers to strenuous effort to make their calling and election sure, rather than revealing to them the final issue of His saving work in the world. (8)

Here Warfield is making three key points. First, he insists that Jesus is not revealing anything about what will finally result from his redemptive mission, but is instead impressing upon his hearers the ethical and spiritual importance of striving to walk the way of discipleship in a time when many are seeking easier paths. And Jesus is saying this to specific people in a particular historical context. He had come as the promised Messiah to his own people, but those to whom he had been sent were not receiving his redemptive mission. Jesus is making it clear, says Warfield, "that salvation is difficult and that it is our duty to address ourselves to obtaining it with diligence and earnest effort" (9).

A closely related point is that Jesus's warning speaks here to a specific historical setting. He is setting his face toward Jerusalem in the knowledge that the success of his mission is not to be ascertained by how he is seen by large crowds of people—either those who cheer him as he enters the city or those who jeer him when he suffers on the way to Calvary.

Another Warfieldian point: these verses do not tell us anything about the course of redemptive history. Is it unthinkable that there ever have been—or ever will be—circumstances in which more people walk the narrow path than travel the broad road that leads to destruction? Is the proportion of saved to unsaved in Jesus's account simply irreversible (15)?

The fact is, Warfield observes, Jesus is fond of imagery where the few become many and the small becomes large. The mustard seed and leaven images illustrate this, and Warfield thinks it is significant that those examples sit in the Gospels "side by side" with the numbers of those who are saved—thus pointing along with the mustard seed and leaven images to how a small beginning "opens out the widest process for the reach of the saving process as time flows on; so wide a prospect as quite to reverse the implications with respect to the ultimate proportions of the saved and the lost" (22).

In the light of these considerations, says Warfield, the case for the small-number perspective "crumbles when subjected to scrutiny." We can be confident, then, that the saving work of Christ "shall embrace the immensely greater part of the human race" (22).

6

Solid Grounding, Confused Theology

IN THE LATE 1970S I SERVED on a panel at a conference at Wheaton College. I forget what the assigned theme for our panel was, but I remember that for some reason I said something in passing about regeneration, and I was immediately corrected in a very public manner by a fellow panelist.

What I said was that we do not have a clear idea of when the Holy Spirit regenerates a person. It could happen years before a discernible conversion takes place in a person's life. In saying that, I was relying primarily on what I had picked up in a seminary course in which we had been assigned readings on Reformed understandings of the *ordo salutis*, and I was operating with this simple scheme in mind: Regeneration is the planting of the seed of new life in the heart of one of God's elect, and the elect person has no role in the seed planting. Once the seed is planted, it begins to grow—that is, the process of sanctification begins. My categories for understanding this were Aristotelian. Just as an acorn when planted begins to grow toward the goal of being a fully actualized oak tree, the initial "new life" that begins this process is invisible from "above ground" until it breaks out into the open in a visible sprouting. In the life of the elect person, that sprouting is when conversion occurs at last—the conscious appropriation of the effects of the new life that was planted in the act of regeneration.

So, that was the scheme that I had in mind when I made my comment about a temporal distance between regeneration and conversion. As providence would have it—a less than kindly providence in this case—sitting next to me on that panel was the great James I. Packer, who calmly remarked that while I was theologically confused, he would not go into it because the topic was not relevant to the theme of our panel.

Afterward, though, Packer did give me some brief (and kindly!) counsel. Knowing my Dutch Calvinist loyalties, he told me to check the Canons of Dort. "Regeneration and conversion go together," he said. "The Spirit's seed-planting is occasioned by the hearing of the Word."

Packer was right about the Canons, of course. Dort clearly depicts conversion and regeneration as two aspects of one co-ordinated work of the Spirit: "When God accomplishes his good pleasure in his elect, or works in them true conversion, he not only causes the gospel to be externally preached to them, and powerfully illuminates their minds by his Holy Spirit, that they may rightly understand and discern the things of the Spirit of God, but by the efficacy of the same regenerating Spirit, he pervades the inmost recesses of the man, he opens the closed and softens the hardened heart, and circumcises that which was uncircumcised."[1]

Having confirmed Packer's counsel to me, I quietly vowed to refrain from ever again declaring anything about such mat-

---

1. Canons of the Synod of Dort, Third and Fourth Heads, article 11, in *The Creeds of Christendom, with a History and Critical Notes*, ed. Philip Schaff, vol. 3 (Grand Rapids: Baker Books, 1996), 590.

ters, which were clearly outside of my own areas of scholarly focus. And I kept this vow for several decades until, early in this century, I cochaired with a Catholic bishop the official Reformed-Catholic dialogue, focusing for two and half years on baptism. While preparing for those discussions, I discovered the Westminster article on children dying in infancy. What especially struck me was that Westminster actually seems to conflict with Dort's insistence that the regeneration of sinners is closely coordinated by the Spirit with the proclamation of the gospel. I realized that I could have used this as a response to Packer. Dying infants do not hear and grasp the message of the gospel, and yet at the very least the Westminster Assembly declared without qualification that the children of elect parents who die in infancy are regenerated by the Spirit of God.

I say Westminster *seems* to contradict Dort, because it is possible to reconcile the two by understanding an implicit "normally" in Dort's account—so that *normally* regeneration happens in coordination with the proclamation of the Word. In fact, the Canons themselves acknowledge that regeneration does take place on occasion apart from the proclamation of the Word, in its article "The Salvation of the Infants of Believers": "Since we must make judgments about God's will from his Word, which testifies that the children of believers are holy, not by nature but by virtue of the gracious covenant in which they together with their parents are included, godly parents ought not to doubt the election and salvation of their children whom God calls out of this life in infancy."[2]

Nor can grieving parents know exactly when the seed planting of regeneration has taken place—at birth, during the child's

2. Canons of the Synod of Dort, First Head of Doctrine, article 17, in Schaff, *The Creeds of Christendom*, 3:585.

baptism, at the time of death, or at some other moment. And the need to allow for mystery in this has been the typical understanding of how it goes in the Calvinist tradition. No Reformed theologian of note has, for example, condemned John Calvin for saying, in his lengthy defense of his view of baptism in the *Institutes*, that John the Baptist was "sanctified in his mother's womb," and then using this example to warn against those who would "impose a law upon God to keep him from sanctifying whom he pleases."[3] After all, Calvin observes at another point, God "keeps his own timetable of regeneration."[4]

The timetable issue became a significant area of theological debate, though, in the Netherlands at the beginning of the twentieth century, particularly due to Abraham Kuyper's controversial understanding of "presumptive regeneration." Kuyper was not content to allow that God might in exceptional cases regenerate a child who had not yet had occasion to grasp the message of salvation. Kuyper normalized that operation by encouraging the believing community to presume that their baptized children were already regenerated.

In so arguing, Kuyper took this "timetable" topic in directions that caused consternation among some of his Calvinist contemporaries when he made things more difficult for those disagreeing with him by going well beyond the application of his ideas to children. He was widely reported to have said, for example, that Saul of Tarsus might already have been regenerated as he witnessed the stoning of Stephen, so that the encounter with Christ on the Damascus road was a "flowering" of a seed planted long before. Kuyper's views stirred enough controversy in his

3. John Calvin, *Institutes of the Christian Religion*, ed. John T. McNeill, trans. F. L. Battles, Library of Christian Classics, vols. 20 and 21 (Philadelphia: Westminster, 1960), 4.16.17, pp. 1340–41.

4. Calvin, *Institutes* 4.16.31, p. 1357.

Dutch denomination that an official theological compromise resolution had to be adopted in 1905.[5]

Kuyper informed his Princeton friends of the issues at stake in those Dutch controversies in an 1891 essay explaining his views on the subject.[6] Kuyper argued that while Calvinists know they can never "pronounce absolutely on the presence or absence of spiritual life in infants," they do have solid theological grounds, given the covenant promises recorded in the Scriptures, for affirming that their infant children are the "recipients of efficacious grace, in whom the work of regeneration proper has already begun" by the divine implanting of the "seed of faith." Thus, according to Calvinist teaching, Kuyper contended, "this consideration based on the divine Word made it imperative [for believers] to look on their infant children as elect and saved and to treat them accordingly."[7] Such was "the import of all Calvinistic confessions, where they treat of the sacraments." And there can be no room for disagreement on the subject within the boundaries of Reformed orthodoxy: "It amounts to a total subversion of the Calvinist view therefore: 1. To deny that the seed of regeneration can be produced by God in a new-born babe. 2. Not to assume this in the case of children of believers. 3. To administer Baptism to them on any other supposition. 4. Not to consider them in bringing them up as potentially regenerated, and not to make this the basis of the

5. "Conclusies van Utrecht, 1905," English translation, in the Christian Reformed Church's *Acts of Synod*, 1942 (Grand Rapids: Christian Reformed Publishing House, 1942), 352. The document is reprinted in Herman Hanko, *For Thy Truth's Sake: A Doctrinal History of the Protestant Reformed Churches* (Grandville, MI: Reformed Free Publishing Co., 2000), 427–31.

6. Abraham Kuyper, "Calvinism," trans. Geerhardus Vos, *Presbyterian and Reformed Review* 2, no. 7 (July 1891): 369–99.

7. Kuyper, "Calvinism," 388.

demand for conversion."[8] Thus Kuyper's controversial teaching regarding "presumptive regeneration"—the insistence that elect parents can take it as given that their children are regenerated either before, or on the occasion of, their baptism as infants.

Kuyper's essay was translated into English by Geerhardus Vos, not too long before Vos departed for the Princeton faculty from the Christian Reformed Church's Theological School in Michigan, where he had been serving as rector. He also published, in the same year Kuyper's essay was published, his own extensive study of the regeneration "timetable" topic,[9] assembling many examples of Calvinist theologians who had used a point similar to Calvin's as support for the doctrine of presumptive regeneration. Vos cites, for example, Beza's statement that while "the hidden judgment must be left to God," we can assume that "*normally, by virtue of the promise, all* who have been born of believing parents, or if one of the parents believes, *are sanctified*," and Peter Martyr's verdict that "we assume that the children of believers are holy, as long as in growing up they do not demonstrate themselves to be estranged from Christ."[10]

Vos pays more attention than Kuyper does to the existence of considerable variations on the "timetable" topic among Reformed thinkers. In so doing, he gives a clear account of the viewpoint that informed the active Dutch opposition to Kuyper's "presumptive regeneration" position, namely, the school of thought that insists that "the usual means by which

8. Kuyper, "Calvinism," 390.

9. Geerhardus Vos, "The Doctrine of the Covenant in Reformed Theology," in *Redemptive History and Biblical Interpretation: The Shorter Writings of Geerhardus Vos*, ed. Richard B. Gaffin Jr. (Phillipsburg, NJ: Presbyterian and Reformed, 1980), 234–67. Vos's address was delivered in Dutch and printed and distributed locally, then translated into English in 1971 and published privately.

10. Vos, "Doctrine of the Covenant," 263–64.

regeneration takes place" is through the proclaimed Word, and "that God does not depart from this rule without necessity." The act of regeneration, on this view, typically "bides its time" in the children of believers "until they can be brought to a conscious possession of the sealed blessings of the covenant."[11]

To repeat, though: Kuyper's opponents did not deny that the Spirit could regenerate children who died before they were capable of grasping the gospel message. Both parties agreed that believing parents whose child died in infancy could be confident that their child is a recipient of God's saving mercies. The argument was about God's "timetable of regeneration" with regard to baptized members of the congregation who move from childhood to adulthood. And, of course, there were worries about too broad an application of the timetable notion beyond pastoral questions about the salvific status of children.

How Much "Epistemic Access"?

In his study of the role of the Holy Spirit in bringing individuals to salvation, the Pentecostal theologian Amos Yong makes an important distinction: the only way for an individual to be saved, he says, is to be "ontologically secured" in salvation through the person and work of Christ. But, says Yong, a person who has not responded knowingly to the message of salvation through Christ can nonetheless be *in* Christ without being "epistemically accessed" to him, through "other providential means of God" than by the actual proclamation by the gospel.[12]

11. Vos, "Doctrine of the Covenant," 264.
12. Amos Yong, *Beyond the Impasse: Toward a Pneumatological Theology of Religions* (Eugene, OR: Wipf & Stock, 2003), 23.

It should be clear by now that Yong's point ought not to worry orthodox Calvinists, since it is simply another way of stating what the Westminster Confession says in the article we have discussed at length. For example, we can assure believing parents whose infant daughter has just died that while their loved one did not develop the capacity to have epistemic access to the claims of the gospel, she is nonetheless ontologically secure in the promises of the covenant for all eternity.

But Yong obviously has adult individuals in mind also, as does Westminster. In addition to dying infants, there are others who do not have epistemic access to the external proclamation of the Word but who are nonetheless ontologically secured in Christ. Both Yong and Westminster obviously are thinking here of persons who live in cultures where the gospel has not yet been proclaimed. Before addressing that category of persons, I must discuss the cultural context where these issues emerge for me in very personal ways: my engagement with individuals in my "Western" setting who have had a measure of epistemic access to the truth claims of the gospel but who either have not given their assent to those claims or articulate their assent in confused, even heretical, ways.

Some in the Calvinist community insist that a person's doctrinal clarity is a crucial—even a necessary—test for ascertaining whether the person is ontologically secure in Christ. No one that I know of has stated this requirement in a more stringent manner than the present-day churchman John MacArthur. In the mid-1990s, a group of us representing evangelicalism and Catholicism issued a document, "Evangelicals and Catholics Together," that was widely viewed as a welcome breakthrough in Catholic-evangelical relations. Several key Calvinist theologians—particularly James Packer and Timothy George—had an important role in drafting some of the significant theological sections. John MacArthur, however, was not pleased, and he publicly condemned the effort. He criticized the evangelicals for saying "that while they believe that the doctrine of justification as articulated by the Reformers is true, they are not willing to say that people must believe it in order to be saved. In other words they believe that people are saved who do not believe the Biblical doctrine of justification."[13]

While I certainly embrace the doctrine of justification by faith alone, I find MacArthur's verdict shockingly restrictive. I was greatly helped in clarifying my own understanding of the doctrine of justification by a thinker who had some typical Catholic qualms about what it represented. In my younger years I had the privilege of getting to know Father Avery Dulles—later Cardinal Dulles—the well-known Jesuit theologian. We had conversations about the doctrine of justification, and he told me that while he thought it was "fine to preach it," he did see dangers that had to be guarded against in doing so. Through our discussions I came to appreciate his cautions about the uses to which we have sometimes put the doctrine.

My appreciation for what I learned from those conversations was reinforced when later I came across this observation by Herman Bavinck: "We must remind ourselves that the Catholic righteousness by good works is vastly preferable to a protestant righteousness by good doctrine. At least righteousness by good works benefits one's neighbor, whereas righteousness by good doctrine only produces lovelessness and pride. Furthermore, we must not blind ourselves to the tremendous faith, genuine repentance, complete surrender and the fervent love

---

13. John MacArthur Jr., *Ashamed of the Gospel: When the Church Becomes like the World* (Wheaton, IL: Crossway Books, 1993), 250.

for God and neighbor evident in the lives and work of many Catholic Christians."[14]

The doctrine of justification by faith was foundational to Bavinck's soteriology. In this observation, however, he was acknowledging that we should recognize the legitimacy of some Catholic qualms about how the Protestant emphasis on the doctrine can play out in practice. He also goes out of his way to commend some of the genuine strengths that he has observed in Catholic life and thought.

I was pleased to find Charles Hodge making a similar conciliatory move in dealing with a theological opponent. Hodge was a stern critic of Friedrich Schleiermacher's theology. When Hodge had studied in Germany in his younger years, he had seen firsthand the dangerous influence of Schleiermacher's rationalist critique of biblical authority. In many ways, Hodge argued, Schleiermacher's thought served to undermine seriously basic tenets of the historic Christian faith.

Reading Hodge on this subject in his *Systematic Theology*, I glanced down to a longish footnote and was surprised at the shift in tone there. He tells how, as a student, he had frequently attended services at Schleiermacher's church. He was taken, he says, by the fact that the hymns sung in those services "were always evangelical and spiritual in an eminent degree, filled with praise and gratitude to our Redeemer." He then reports that one of Schleiermacher's colleagues had told him that often in the evenings the theologian would call his family together, saying: "Hush, children; let us sing a hymn of praise to Christ." And then Hodge adds this tribute to Schleiermacher, who had been dead for a few decades at the time: "Can we doubt that he is

14. Herman Bavinck, *The Certainty of Faith*, trans. Harry der Nederlanden (St. Catharines, ON: Paideia, 1980), 37.

singing those praises now? To whomever Christ is God, St. John assures us, Christ is a Saviour."[15]

Another nineteenth-century advocate of Calvinist orthodoxy, W. G. T. Shedd, in the preface to his book defending the Westminster Standards, asks his readers to consider a person whose doctrinal position we may see as seriously departing from sound theology but who in his "person may be different in his spirit and intention from the nature and tendency of his doctrine." To illustrate his concern, Shedd cites with approval what the poet Coleridge said to a friend who advocated Unitarian beliefs. "I make the greatest difference between ans and isms," Coleridge told his friend. "I should deal insincerely with you, if I said that I thought that Unitarianism is Christianity; but God forbid that I should doubt that you and many other Unitarians are in a practical sense very good Christians."[16]

Given the state of Unitarianism today, we might be surprised by Shedd's joining Coleridge in seeming to go easy on that movement. But in Shedd's time there were Unitarians who gave evidence of having a vital faith in Christ. Ellen Tucker Emerson, the daughter of Ralph Waldo Emerson, stands out for me as an intriguing case in point.[17] She taught Sunday school for most of her adult life at Concord's First Unitarian Church and held Bible studies (from which her father absented himself!) in the

15. Charles Hodge, *Systematic Theology*, vol. 2 (Peabody, MA: Hendrickson, 2003), 440n1.

16. William G. T. Shedd, *Calvinism Pure and Mixed: A Defence of the Westminster Standards* (Carlisle, PA: Banner of Truth Trust, 1986), ix–x.

17. While doing research in 1997 on Ralph Waldo Emerson in the Concord, Massachusetts, Free Public Library, I came across a collection of the correspondence of Emerson's daughter Ellen. My brief account of her here is based on notes taken then, and used for an article I wrote about her, "The Women at the Concord Tombs," *Books and Culture*, January-February 1999, https://www.booksandculture.com/articles/1999/janfeb/9b1034.html.

Emerson home. "All four of us took hold and studied Galatians Saturday evening," she reported in a letter written in 1882, "and with Uncle George we read Romans xi on Sunday evening. That was glorious!"

Ellen had a practical approach to her faith, to which she gave frequent expression in her extensive correspondence. She believed that Jesus was the Savior sent from heaven—not quite a member of the Godhead but of a status higher than the angels—and that a person needed to trust in his atoning work in order to be saved. One of her favorite spiritual books was *The Spirit of St. Francis de Sales*. She also held Dwight L. Moody in high esteem, and often complained about preachers who portrayed Jesus as just another gifted moral teacher.

I accept these examples—Schleiermacher and Miss Emerson—as persons who show signs of a genuine Christ-centered spiritual vitality while falling short of standards of traditional orthodoxy in how they explain their faith. And I take encouragement from the stated views of Bavinck, Hodge, and Shedd in supporting that view. Now, however, I will push the application of Amos Yong's distinction a step further.

Muslims Loving Jesus?

The topic of an interfaith panel in Washington, DC, was "Muslims and Jesus." One of the Muslim panelists described himself as "a Muslim follower of Jesus." He was, he assured us, a devout Muslim. But, he testified, as a member of an interfaith Bible study group, he also regularly reads the gospel accounts of the life of Jesus. The New Testament, he said, has become an important part of his life because Jesus has added a dimension to his deeply held Muslim beliefs by teaching him lessons about love and forgiveness. Because of Jesus, he testified, "I have become a more loving and forgiving Muslim."

The audience for this panel was predominantly evangelical, and when the discussion was opened up for questions, someone immediately challenged the Muslim panelist: "But you Muslims deny the reality of the work of the Cross! How can you say you follow Jesus when you deny what the New Testament says about his atoning work?"

The Muslim responded with an almost pleading tone: "Why do you Christian folks always go immediately to that topic? Yes, we Muslims have questions about whether the crucifixion of Jesus really happened. But why is that such a big deal for you?" Then he pointed to the person next to him, an evangelical missionary to the Middle East: "Look, my Christian friend here has been preaching to Muslims about the cross for ten years, and what are his results? About six converts—six people in ten years! Now, if he had encouraged Muslims to read the Gospels to learn from Jesus about how Muslims can be more forgiving and loving he would have thousands of Muslim people reading the New Testament!"

Hearing that man speak on a panel is certainly no basis for offering an assessment of the state of his soul. But it is not inconceivable to me that these days a Muslim might offer that kind of testimony: regular reading of gospel accounts; a sense of personal connectedness to Jesus, seeing Jesus as teaching him important lessons about love and forgiveness; and in all of this continuing to identify as a devout Muslim.

Here is my basic take on this kind of case. The person may have a genuine experience of the love of Christ without properly understanding what it is about Jesus's person and ministry that makes that love possible. In such an instance, the Christian response should not be to express doubt about the person's testimony about learning forgiveness and love from Jesus. Rather, the focus should be on how to best understand who Jesus is and what he accomplished in his earthly mission.

This is the spiritual journey for many of us: going from being ontologically grounded without epistemic access to gradually grasping the full claims of the gospel. As a Kuyperian, I remain agnostic about when the mystery of regeneration took place in my life, but I do have a vivid memory of Mrs. VandeVusse, my first Sunday school teacher at First Holland Reformed Church in Passaic, New Jersey, teaching us four-year-olds to sing: "Into my heart / into my heart / come into my heart, Lord Jesus. / Come in today / come in to stay / Come into my heart, Lord Jesus." I remember singing those words with a deep sincerity, and then feeling assured afterward that Jesus had done exactly what I had asked him to do. At the time I had no understanding yet of what Jesus had accomplished on my behalf that made it possible for him to be a loving and abiding presence in my life. Mrs. VandeVusse had not prepared us for his entrance into our hearts by teaching us about the substitutionary atonement. But I had the ontological grounding in Christ—I knew his loving embrace—even though I did not yet have the epistemic access to what makes that grounding possible.

None of this is intended to discount the crucial importance of detailed theological understanding of our salvific status. If the Muslim panelist is genuinely grounded in Christ, there will come a time, either here or in eternity, when he will need to gain epistemic access to what was accomplished on his behalf at Calvary. Everyone who belongs to Jesus will eventually "see him as he is," which includes worshiping him as the Lamb who was slain. In the meantime, those of us who believe we have access to the profound truths of the gospel do well to allow for the working of the Spirit where those truths are not yet fully appropriated in a person's life.

To understand the kinds of cases I have briefly described—Schleiermacher, Ellen Emerson, the Muslim panelist—it is important to seek to discern signs that persons are reaching beyond, or as far as they can within their life circumstances, the categories presently accessible to them. I find Kuyper doing this with liberal theologians as he nears the end of his Stone Lectures. Like Hodge on Schleiermacher, Kuyper was often aggressive in pointing out the dangers of modernist theology. But as he concludes his presentations at Princeton Seminary, he takes on a gentler tone about modernists. While expressing dismay about the way many theologians of his day deny Christ's divinity, he remarks that they nonetheless push as far as they can within their understanding of Jesus's exclusive humanity to have him "continue to glitter from the throne of humanity, as the highest ideal of the modernized human heart." Because of this, Kuyper warns, the orthodox Christian "who would look down upon such men, would only dishonor himself."[18]

These kinds of cases confirm the old saw that a person's actual faith may be better than the person's theology. That saying, however, applies more often to individuals than to communities. There may still be individual Unitarians who love key elements of the gospel as Ellen Emerson did, but there probably are not many Unitarian Sunday school classes with teachers like her. When a robust Trinitarian theology slips into Arianism, some hearts may still hold a strong devotion to Jesus Christ as ranked somewhere above the angels, but history makes it clear that in their community he will, as it were, keep slipping down the ontological scale.

18. Abraham Kuyper, *Lectures on Calvinism: Six Lectures Delivered at Princeton University under Auspices of the L. P. Stone Foundation* (Grand Rapids: Eerdmans, 1931), 181.

Solid theology—formulated with careful attention to heresies that deceive and confuse—is essential to sustaining a shared vibrant faith. This is a point I have pushed hard with my conversation partners during two decades of extensive Mormon-evangelical dialogue. Each year we have met twice for two-day discussions. From the start we have concentrated on central theological issues, dealing with the basic question of how we human beings can be in a right relationship with God. This has resulted in intensive discussions about sin and grace, atonement, biblical authority, ecclesiology, and related matters.

We often discussed at length together the way some Mormon thinkers portray the Fall in Genesis 3 in felix culpa terms. In eating the forbidden fruit, that argument goes, our first parents took a positive step forward in human development. We evangelicals strongly opposed this perspective, insisting that the serpent's promise that by ignoring the divine prohibition they would become "as gods" was a Satanic lie.

We were puzzled by the sense that our Mormon friends seemed to want it both ways: the Fall was both a positive step and a tragedy. Finally one of our Mormon participants offered an interesting illustration. The "good Fall" theme, he said, is for Mormons only one strand in a theological concert—something like the soprano or alto lines in a fine musical composition. But what is missed when we hear only these voices, he said, are the bass and tenor parts, which sing of our desperate need for a Savior. Without the atoning work of Christ we are endlessly "lost," and no amount of good works can rescue us from the bondage of sin. He then quoted a passage from the Book of Mormon where the utter tragedy of the Fall means that

> our spirits must become subject to that angel who fell from
> before the presence of the Eternal God, and became the

devil, to rise no more. And our spirits must have become like unto him, and we become devils, angels to a devil, to be shut out from the presence of our God, and to remain with the father of lies, in misery, like unto himself. . . . O how great the goodness of our God, who prepareth a way for our escape from the grasp of this awful monster; yea, that monster, death and hell, which I call the death of the body, and also the death of the spirit. (2 Nephi 9:7–10)

The theological themes my Mormon friend highlighted in this message were not new to me. In over twenty years of formal theological conversations, as well as in seminar discussions with students at Brigham Young and in conversations with church officials in Salt Lake City, I consistently heard this "bass/tenor" voice. And Latter-day Saints regularly sing in that voice in their local worship gatherings. As I write this, the most frequently sung hymn at weekly Mormon "sacrament meetings" is "I Stand All Amazed," which could be sung with equal spiritual passion in any Calvinist congregation:

> I stand all amazed at the love Jesus offers me,
> Confused at the grace that so fully he proffers me.
> I tremble to know that for me he was crucified,
> That for me, a sinner, he suffered, he bled and died.
>
> *Chorus*
>
> Oh, it is wonderful that he should care for me
> Enough to die for me!
> Oh, it is wonderful, wonderful to me!
>
> I marvel that he would descend from his
>   throne divine
> To rescue a soul so rebellious and proud as mine,

That he should extend his great love unto such as I,
Sufficient to own, to redeem, and to justify.

I think of his hands pierced and bleeding
   to pay the debt!
Such mercy, such love and devotion can I forget?
No, no, I will praise and adore at the mercy seat,
Until at the glorified throne I kneel at his feet.[19]

I am impressed with my Mormon scholar friend's email explanation regarding the "base/tenor" lines about sin and grace. But I still worry that those themes are played out in a larger "doctrinal symphony" in which the alto and soprano sections depict the Fall as an occasion of human growth and as a journey of self-actualization. The two story lines spell out two quite different understandings of what it means for human beings to flourish in God-honoring ways. The difficulty here is very similar to the Schleiermacher-type case where the person's understanding of the gospel expressed in, say, the hymns the person loves to sing stands in tension with the person's epistemic theological formulations. Holding on to a deep faith in Christ may be sustainable within one's personal life, but it does not lend itself to being passed from one generation to another. The liberal theologians commended by Kuyper, as in Schleiermacher's personal piety, are stabilized in their individual lives by the continuing influence of what has been believed in the past, as well as by the spiritual impact of the past, and by practices that may be continued even though they draw their strength from an orthodoxy that has now been abandoned. Similarly,

19. "I Stand All Amazed," The Church of Jesus Christ of Latter-day Saints, accessed April 10, 2023, https://www.churchofjesuschrist.org/music/text/hymns/i-stand-all-amazed?lang=eng.

while a Mormon who knows the whole symphony but chooses to sing primarily in the bass/tenor voices may be influenced by deeply personal experiences, none of this is easy to pass on to a generation that lacks the means of collective sustainability. It is significant that the apostle addresses the mandate to be able to "give the reason for the hope that you have" to a *community* that he has already urged to be "like-*minded*" (1 Pet. 3:15, 8).

Still, the examples I have touched upon here do—as I see things—support the idea that a person can be genuinely grounded in Christ ontologically without having adequate epistemic access to the truth claims that provide the explanatory basis for that grounding. But now I must address the cases of persons who are grounded ontologically in Christ without any epistemic access at all to the claims of the gospel—that category identified by the Westminster divines as "elect persons who are incapable of being outwardly called by the ministry of the Word."

Expanding the Categories

W. G. T. Shedd was willing to acknowledge "broad and liberal" salvific implications in Westminster's affirmation regarding "all other elect persons." It is significant that he and his Princeton friends would devote theological attention to that topic, since the "elect infants" part was at the center of the denominational debate. They simply could have let that additional phrasing stand without further commentary. It is a given in Reformed theology, for example, that large numbers of Old Testament saints were saved on the basis of the atoning mercies that would be accomplished by Christ, even though they did not have epistemic access to the proclamation of the claims of the gospel. And it had long been taken for granted by Calvinists that there are elect adults who do not have the cognitive capacities to understand the message of salvation.

Shedd, however, did not refrain from looking at the more expansive category of elect persons among the unevangelized. Westminster, he declared early in his book, gives us nothing that "denies the possibility of the salvation of any sinner on earth who feels his sin, and trusts in the sacrifice of Christ in case he has heard of it, or *would* trust in it if he should hear of it. [The Confession] does not teach that no heathen is or can be saved."[20] He came back to this topic later, arguing that the Confession encourages us to believe that "some of the elect are regenerated by an *extraordinary* method from among the unevangelized, and without the written word."[21]

The possibility of the salvific category that Shedd was allowing for in these comments had already been established by his Princeton friends. A. A. Hodge had made it clear in 1869 that he had no theological problem with the salvation of "infants and others not capable of being called by the gospel"—but without getting into any specifics about the "others." At that point he just acknowledged that the Confession allows that some individuals—adults as well as children—are simply "regenerated and sanctified immediately by God without the use of means."[22] Then shortly before his death in 1886—as the revisionist controversies were heating up—Hodge repeated his conviction with a clear allusion to article 3, creating room for cases that went beyond those already acknowledged by traditional Calvinists: "Through [Christ's] atonement not only all adult believers, but all dying in infancy, all idiots [*sic*] *and all who have been saved by*

20. Shedd, *Calvinism Pure and Mixed*, 22.
21. Shedd, *Calvinism Pure and Mixed*, 59.
22. A. A. Hodge, *The Confession of Faith* (Carlisle, PA: Banner of Truth Trust, 1958), 174–75.

any extraordinary means known only to God, are reconciled to God and stand absolved from guilt."[23]

Warfield was less inclined than either Shedd or A. A. Hodge to move from his affirmation of the election of all children who die in infancy to any explicit application of the Westminster article to adults who have not had access to the Word. Indeed, in his *Are They Few That Be Saved?* essay, he makes a point of distancing himself from Shedd on this particular matter.[24] But he does this briefly in passing, and then immediately affirms that "the immensely greater part of the human race" will be saved in the end. Then he expresses his general sense of theological solidarity with Shedd as he appeals to his great respect for "such honored names among prophets of our own as Charles Hodge, Robert L. Dabney and William G. T. Shedd."

While Warfield, A. A. Hodge, and Shedd certainly disagreed among themselves about some theological specifics, they clearly shared a common desire to advocate for a Calvinism that was guided by a spirit of salvific generosity. The debate over elect infants provided them with the occasion to demonstrate that this spirit of generosity was perfectly compatible with a nonnegotiable commitment to sovereign electing grace as the only hope for human beings otherwise lost in their depraved condition.

They knew that many of the revisionists were intent on ridding the church of foundational traditional beliefs rather than simply wanting to clarify the intentions of the Confession. For Warfield and company, then, the Declaratory Statement of 1903 was an important victory, in that it offered guidance on how

23. A. A. Hodge, *Evangelical Theology: Lectures on Doctrine* (Carlisle, PA: Banner of Truth Trust, 1976), 218 (emphasis added).

24. Benjamin Warfield, *Are They Few That Be Saved?* (New York: Our Hope Publications, 1918), n. 39. The PDF of this booklet, accessible, with no pagination, is at https://reformed.org/eschaton/few_saved.pdf.

the church should understand the article in question without requiring any confessional revision. In doing so, the Statement maintained the Confession's strong emphasis on human depravity and divine sovereignty, in a way that also clearly expressed a spirit of salvific generosity.

Shedd in particular pushed the generosity topic more aggressively than did his Princeton friends, but always while demonstrating his firm commitment to the unique features of Calvinist soteriology. He regularly reminded his readers that he was not suggesting that the unevangelized are elected on the basis of virtuous traits they have cultivated, or because of a positive response to the dictates of natural law. If any unevangelized are saved, it is by sovereign grace alone. In pushing this emphasis, he insisted that the elect among the unevangelized will of necessity demonstrate signs of their election in their inner lives. Here is how Shedd describes the way in which regeneration takes place in the life of a person who has not heard the gospel proclaimed:

> The Divine Spirit exerts his regenerating grace, . . . making use of conscience, or "the law written on the heart," as the means of convicting of sin preparatory to importing the new divine life. . . . And since regeneration in the instance of the adult immediately produces faith and repentance, a regenerate heathen is both a believer and penitent. He feels sorrow for sin, and the need of mercy. This felt need of mercy and desire for it is potentially and virtually faith in the Redeemer. For although the Redeemer has not been presented to him historically and personally as the object of faith, yet the Divine Spirit by the new birth has wrought in him the sincere and longing disposition to believe in him.[25]

25. Shedd, *Calvinism Pure and Mixed*, 128–29.

In one sense that is a remarkable passage, coming from someone widely regarded as possessing impeccable Calvinist credentials (and in a book published by the Banner of Truth Trust!). However, Shedd is simply following closely what the Canons of Dort say will characterize the inner life of an elect person: "a true faith in Christ, filial fear, a godly sorrow for sin, [and] a hungering and thirsting after righteousness."[26] Shedd is not denying that "a true faith in Christ" is essential for salvation, but he is allowing that such faith can manifest itself in an elect person's life as "potentially and virtually faith in the Redeemer" who "has not been presented to him historically and personally." This comports well with how the writer to the Hebrews characterizes the faith of Moses, who "considered abuse suffered for the Christ to be greater wealth than the treasures of Egypt" (Heb. 11:26 NRSV).

Bavinckian Support

Given my own Dutch neo-Calvinist commitments, I can't refrain here from observing that during this same period Herman Bavinck expressed in his *Reformed Dogmatics* a sense of mystery about the scope of God's electing mercies: "In light of Scripture, both with regard to the salvation of pagans and that of children who die in infancy, we cannot get beyond abstaining from a firm judgment, in either a positive or a negative sense." Then Bavinck quotes from the Westminster Confession's "Of Effectual Calling" article as confirming his sense of mystery regarding God's electing purposes.[27]

26. Canons of the Synod of Dort, First Head of Doctrine, article 12, in Schaff, *The Creeds of Christendom*, 3:583–84.
27. Herman Bavinck, *Reformed Dogmatics*, ed. John Bolt, trans. John Vriend, vol. 4 (Grand Rapids: Baker Academic, 2004), 726.

For Bavinck, God's generosity extends even into the eschaton. In his critique of the "single decree" conception of the supralapsarians, in the second volume of his *Reformed Dogmatics*, he contends that it is not theologically proper "to say that in the eternal state of the lost, God *exclusively* reveals his justice, and that in that of the elect he *exclusively* reveals his mercy. Also in the church purchased as it was by the blood of his Son, God's justice becomes manifest." And then he immediately adds this verdict: "and also in the place of perdition there are degrees of punishment and glimmerings of his mercy."[28] And lest we miss the point he is making, he repeats it three pages later: "It is not true that God's justice can only be manifested in the wretched state of the lost and his mercy only in the blessedness of the elect, for in heaven, too, his justice and holiness are radiantly present, and even in hell there is still some evidence of his mercy and goodness."[29]

I am not clear about how all of that works out in Bavinck's mind. But it does strike me as the kind of expression of mystery that some Calvinists typically fall back on when they want to correct impressions of theological harshness. Here, for example, is one of those fall-back expressions from Charles Hodge. Having made a point of insisting that God's justice does not allow for good works performed by an unbeliever to count toward salvific mercy in the eyes of God, Hodge tells readers to keep in mind that God is both "a righteous ruler and a just judge." This means that "we have the assurance which runs through the Scriptures, that 'The judge of all the earth' must 'do right.' (Gen. xviii. 25.) 'God is a righteous judge.' (Ps. vii. 11, marginal reading.) 'He shall judge the world with righteousness.' (Ps. xcvi. 13.)

---

28. Herman Bavinck, *Reformed Dogmatics*, ed. John Bolt, trans. John Vriend, vol. 2 (Grand Rapids: Baker Academic, 2004), 386.

29. Bavinck, *Reformed Dogmatics*, 2:389.

'Clouds and darkness are round about Him: righteousness and judgment are the habitation of his throne.' (Ps. xcvii. 2.) Notwithstanding all the apparent inequalities in the distribution of his favours; notwithstanding the prosperity of the wicked and the afflictions of the righteous, the conviction is everywhere expressed that God is just."[30] Hodge sticks to generality in making his fallback statement: God will eventually make it clear that he will "do right" in his dealings with humankind, while Bavinck gets more specific: "even in hell" there will be clear signs of the Lord's "mercy and goodness."

These are awkward matters to articulate with theological precision. What is obvious, though, is that both Bavinck and Hodge are refusing simply to stay silent on a concern that looms large for many of us in the Calvinist tradition. What is the Lord's disposition toward those who seemingly are incapable of separating the claims of the gospel from brutal treatment by people whom they identify with Christianity? Here is an instance that has troubled me since I first read about it in a news report.[31] During the "ethnic cleansing" campaign in Bosnia-Herzegovina in the 1990s, some soldiers—described as members of a "Christian" military force—raped a young Muslim woman. While they engaged in their wicked business, her baby began to cry and she pleaded with them to leave her alone so that she might nurse her child. One of the soldiers responded by grabbing her baby, cutting its head off and placing it on her breast.

A horrible story. We can certainly understand how the Muslim woman would experience not only much sustained grief

30. Charles Hodge, *Systematic Theology*, vol. 1 (Peabody, MA: Hendrickson, 2003), 307.

31. I discussed this story in relationship to common grace theology in my *He Shines in All That's Fair: Culture and Common Grace* (Grand Rapids: Eerdmans, 2002), 42.

and shame throughout her life but would also nurture a deep personal hostility toward anything associated with Christianity. Don't we also have good theological reasons for believing that God deeply understands her grief and shame—and her hostility toward Christianity? And we must remember that on the Old Princeton theologians' interpretation of the Westminster Confession, the Muslim woman is the mother of an elect child who is now with Jesus in heaven. Surely, I want to say, there are matters at stake here that touch the heart of God, and that, using Hodge's formulation, "somehow and somewhere" the righteous Judge of the universe will do what is right by this woman and her elect child. For us, the best thing is to follow the apostle Paul's example and to pause in struggling to find the right theological formulation and start singing words of faith in the mysteries of God's ways with human beings:

> O the depth of the riches and wisdom and knowledge of God! How unsearchable are his judgments and how inscrutable his ways!
>
> > "For who has known the mind of the Lord?
> > > Or who has been his counselor?"
> > "Or who has given a gift to him,
> > > to receive a gift in return?"
>
> For from him and through him and to him are all things. To him be the glory forever. Amen. (Rom. 11:33–36 NRSV)

7

Seeking an Unknown God

A PASTOR CALLED ME ABOUT a difficult funeral service he was facing. A single mother in his inner-city congregation had been asking for prayer during the past year for her son Dennis (not his real name), who was in his late teens. He had, as his mother regularly put it, "gotten in with the wrong crowd," and she was sure he was engaging in criminal activity. Recently, though, she had reported that the Lord seemed to be answering the prayers for Dennis, who had come to his mother to tell her that he had gotten into some bad patterns and now wanted to change his ways. Tearfully, he thanked his mother for praying for him and asked her to keep doing so.

She was thrilled. But now, the pastor told me, her hopes were shattered. Shortly after his talk with Dennis's mother, Dennis had been killed in his group's armed burglary attempt. In a few days my pastor friend would be conducting Dennis's funeral service. "I'm having a hard time thinking straight about it," he said. "What can I possibly say in a service of this sort?"

I told him that my sense was that the one positive thing that the pastor could build upon was the spirit of Dennis's recent conversation with his mother. The pastor said he would think about how to focus on that. I also told him that I would be praying that the Lord would give him wisdom, and I asked that he call me after the funeral to tell me how it went.

I was impressed by his report to me. It was a rough service, he said, but he was able to offer words of hope. It was no small thing, he had told the gathering, that Dennis had expressed sorrow over his recent activities and had asked his mother for her continuing prayers. What Dennis was doing in that conversation, the pastor had said, was acknowledging both his mother's authority over him and God's supreme authority over her. This was a sign that Dennis, in the midst of much personal brokenness and confusion, was in effect looking for a way to honor God's purposes for human life— an important step in the direction of faith. Yes, Dennis had not yet succeeded in repairing his life. But his conversation with his mother should now be accepted as a gift from the Lord. It gives us hope as we now give Dennis over to the divine mercies.

That event happened several decades ago, but I still think about the theological issues involved—most of them having a clear connection to what I have been discussing here. I once told the Dennis story to a class of seminarians, and one of them responded: "I can't help but think that God liked what he saw when Dennis talked to his mom about wanting to change the pattern of his life!" I agreed with that assessment, but I think we have to consider going further. It could be that God was not just looking down on Dennis and appreciating what the young man was confessing about his present situation. As a Calvinist, I want to think, not so much about what the Lord is *seeing* in Dennis's life, but what God is *doing* there.

"Fruits of Election"

Recently I have been studying the official twentieth-century Catholic documents that I cited earlier, on non-Christian religions. One of them, *Nostra Aetate*, issued in 1965, was received as a groundbreaking document on the relationship of Christianity with the major non-Christian religions: Islam, Hinduism, and Buddhism were mentioned by name, and of particular significance were several paragraphs with a conciliatory tone about Catholic-Jewish relations.[1]

The issues had been addressed more briefly a year earlier, in *Lumen Gentium*, which was a declaration on the mission of the Catholic Church in the world. What was significant about that document was that it referred also in broader terms to practitioners of indigenous folk religions, "those who in shadows and images seek the unknown God." The Lord, said the bishops, does not remain "far distant" from this portion of humankind:

> Those also can attain to salvation who through no fault of their own do not know the Gospel of Christ or His Church, yet sincerely seek God and moved by grace strive by their deeds to do His will as it is known to them through the dictates of conscience. Nor does Divine Providence deny the helps necessary for salvation to those who, without blame on their part, have not yet arrived at an explicit knowledge of God and with His grace strive to live a good life. Whatever

---

1. Declaration on the Relation of the Church to Non-Christian Religions, *Nostra Aetate*, Proclaimed by His Holiness, Pope Paul VI, on October 28, 1965, https://www.vatican.va/archive/hist_councils/ii_vatican_council/documents/vat-ii_decl_19651028_nostra-aetate_en.html.

good or truth is found amongst them is looked upon by the Church as a preparation for the Gospel.[2]

I find this account of the possibility of salvation without access to the gospel message to be quite weak theologically. For one thing, it applies to people generically, that they can manage to "attain to salvation" even though they, "through no fault of their own," have no epistemic access to the Christian message. This contrasts to the Calvinist view that an individual is elected by God, not because of the person's innate capacities or on the basis of an individual choice to perform good works, but by God's salvific gracious initiative toward that individual.

The grace referred to in the Vatican declaration, then, is a nonsalvific *prevenient* grace. It is, again, a generic gift to all human beings that allows them to choose for salvation, at which point persons receive access to the saving grace that takes hold in their lives through the church's sacramental ministries.

What is missing in the Catholic formulations is the strong pneumatological emphasis that characterizes the Calvinist perspective. In Shedd's way of putting the case, as we have seen, if a person from an unevangelized culture is one of the elect, it is because of the Holy Spirit's initiative of creating in that person a sorrow for sin and a yearning for the righteousness that is only possible to attain through the atoning work of Christ.

Back to Dennis, then. The hope that the pastor could offer Dennis's loved ones focused on the penitent spirit Dennis exhibited in his conversation with his mother and his expression of a deep desire to change his ways. The "ontological" question

2. Dogmatic Constitution on the Church, *Lumen Gentium*, Solemnly Promulgated by His Holiness, Pope Paul VI, on November 21, 1964, chap. 2, section 16, http://www.vatican.va/archive/hist_councils/ii_vatican_council /documents/vat-ii_const_19641121_lumen-gentium_en.html.

in his case is whether those expressed concerns were grounded (using the Dortian wording) in "a godly sorrow for sin" and "a hungering and thirsting after righteousness." We cannot know whether that is the case—just as we cannot know for certain what is going on in the heart of a person in an isolated Borneo village who shows a spirit of penitence. But expressions of guilt and a desire for life-changing patterns of behavior are hopeful signs from a Calvinist perspective.

Praying in Hope

I do like the language, though, that the Catholic bishops used in introducing the category of practitioners of indigenous folk religions. These are people, they said, "who in shadows and images seek the unknown God." The bishops were right in using the image from Acts 17, where the apostle Paul engaged in dialogue with pagan philosophers in Athens. The unevangelized world is full of the "shadows and images" in the quest for an unknown God. That imagery, however, also increasingly applies as well to our own Western culture.

I have "pagan" friends whom I spend time with frequently. If the culture in which they were raised could still be thought of as broadly "Christian" or "Judeo-Christian," they missed most of the signals. They know nothing about the Bible or about the history of the church. Nor do they seem to have any interest in learning about such things. Because we are friends, though, they do occasionally express puzzlement about my identification with the Christian faith, even though they basically seem to like me in spite of all that. Recently one of them faced some difficult family issues, and I told her she would be in my thoughts and prayers. Later she sent me an email telling me that while she does not believe in prayer, she did feel like there were "good vibes" coming from me that were helping her get through her crisis.

I do regularly pray for these friends. Included in what I say to God about them is my gratitude for the good things in their lives. They have a strong sense of justice. They are impressively kind people. They love beautiful things. In fact, it is precisely because of these commitments that they think of Christianity—and evangelical Christianity in particular—as "toxic." I do not actively attempt to evangelize them. I try simply to be a friend whom they can trust, while also trying occasionally to plant thoughts that counter their negative stereotypes. And again, I pray for them. I ask God to work in their hearts, transforming the things that I like about them into the genuine yearnings that can serve as evidence of saving grace in their lives. But there is more that I do in my prayers for them. I work at having faith on their behalf—something that I will now try to explain theologically.

Faith on Behalf Of?

My predecessor in the presidency of Fuller Seminary, David Hubbard, was one of the important mentors in my academic career. I served as his provost for three years, and then for one year as president-elect while he was still in office. He schooled me—like him, I was a reluctant administrator—in many of the practical details of seminary leadership. Fortunately, he also managed to slip in some formative theological lessons.

One of the most memorable happened during a fund-raising talk. David was not fond of giving those talks, but he compensated by making sure they doubled as lessons in biblical teaching. On this occasion he chose to reflect on the account in Luke 5 where some men took a paralytic friend to Jesus to be healed. However, when they arrived at the place where Jesus was teaching, the huge crowd made it impossible to carry their friend close to the Savior. So they made a hole in the roof tiles and lowered their friend's body down into Jesus's presence.

Hubbard said that one thing that has puzzled him as an academic administrator about this story is: Who paid to repair the roof? We often think, he said, of the more dramatic aspects of supporting the work of the kingdom, but practical costs also typically have to be dealt with: replacing light bulbs, fixing furniture, plumbing work, repairing roofs.

The donors Hubbard was addressing obviously loved the point he was making—several of them expressed the hope afterward that their contributions would be used for maintenance-type needs. As he was speaking to the group, Hubbard could tell that he had connected with them on donor issues, so he used the moment to broach more serious theological issues. Hubbard observed that the paralytic man's friends had not been put off by the practical obstacles they faced in bringing him to Jesus for healing, so Jesus commended them for this. Hubbard quoted from Luke's narrative: "When he saw their faith, he said, 'Friend, your sins are forgiven you'" (Luke 5:20 NRSV). Then Hubbard tossed out a comment that I have ever since wanted to discuss with him at length. This is one of those occasions, he said, where the Bible points us to a mystery: Jesus not only healed the paralytic man, but when he saw the faith of the man's friends, he forgave the paralytic's sins. While this is never spelled out in great detail, it is clear—and Hubbard also cited 1 Corinthians 7:14: "For the unbelieving husband is made holy through his wife" (NRSV)—that God honors our efforts to have faith *on behalf of others.*

In thinking much since then about what Hubbard said, I apply it to Dennis's relationship with his mother. Could it be that the Lord not only *rejoiced* in Dennis's mother's diligent prayers on her son's behalf, but that he *honored her faith* on her son's behalf? Might it also be that we can do more (but not less!) than pray for the spread of the gospel to presently unreached people groups—that if we pray for individuals in those cultures who are experiencing in their hearts inklings that they are not directing their lives in the right way, that the Holy Spirit will see and honor our faith on their behalf? And could it even be that God will honor my efforts to have faith on behalf of my unbelieving friends?

Here is a real case where I have hope that something like that actually happened. Sarah (not her real name) was raised in an evangelical home and was abused by her father, who was regarded as a "saint" in the Christian community. She rebelled against her Christian upbringing, engaging in a promiscuous lifestyle. Those of us who knew her story prayed for her, but with an awareness that her sense of violation by her dad and his Christian admirers ran so deep that she seemed psychologically incapable of acknowledging a faith in Christ. There came a time, though, when she admitted to herself that she was addicted to alcohol, and she joined Alcoholics Anonymous (AA). As she later reported it to some of us, the hardest part of her AA participation was the group practice of praying the Lord's Prayer at the beginning of meetings. For the first year or so, she refused to join in with the prayer. There came a point, however, when she began to utter the words of the prayer—but only, she says, as a way of identifying with the group. She does find AA's insistence on giving one's will over to a "Higher Power" a necessary step in her recovery, but she insists on keeping that concept rather imprecise in her mind. And that is pretty much where she is today.

I draw a parallel between her journey and what was going on with Dennis at the end of his life. We Christians who know this woman do see significant changes having occurred in her journey. It certainly makes sense to sympathize with her deep disillusionment with the kind of Christianity she knew in her youth. It also seems right to thank the Lord for how her AA experience has served to bring transformation into her life.

Is there more? I hope so. I am theologically open to the real possibility that the prayers of her friends have been answered salvifically. The profound changes that have occurred in her life seem to have continuities with the sorts of things that come from a conversion experience. Could it be that the Spirit is at work in her decision finally to utter the words of the Lord's Prayer, even though she does not acknowledge actually meaning all of the words? Is it possible that as she has surrendered her will to her "Higher Power," she is in reality *being reached out to* by "the Spirit, who worketh when, and where, and how he pleaseth"? I think so, and I am convinced that the case can be made with some theological substance.

8

Blessing the Nations

A CONVERSATION THAT I HAD in China with a young woman, a recent convert to Christianity, has had a lasting theological impact on me.[1] I was lecturing at several seminaries on the Chinese mainland, and Melissa had been assigned to me as my translator. When we first met she told me with obvious enthusiasm that she had encountered Christ a few years before, and her relationship with him was now the center of her life. Melissa also said that she was eager to learn more about theology, and she was looking forward to translating my lectures as helping to fulfill that goal.

Melissa's mastery of English was impressive, and she clearly was highly intelligent. In lecture situations where I need a translator, I typically get some sense of how good the translator is by the clarity and relevance of the questions and comments posed to me in the discussion period. She was obviously doing a fine job.

On our final day together, she asked if she could talk to me about a personal theological concern. I agreed, and when

---

1. I am expanding here on a brief telling of this story in my *All That God Cares About: Common Grace and Divine Delight* (Grand Rapids: Brazos, 2020).

we began that conversation she seemed on the verge of tears. Melissa had been raised in a devout Buddhist family, she said, and her parents were not happy when she became a Christian. What bothered them the most was the Christian teaching that salvation comes only through Christ. Revering ancestors was a key element in her family's religious culture, she said, and her parents were deeply offended by the thought that their daughter's newfound faith included the belief that all of her ancestors were condemned to hell.

Then the tears came, along with a pleading tone: "Revering my ancestors means much to me, and I want to assure my parents that I have no desire to dishonor my family heritage. So please tell me what I as a Christian can say to my parents about this!"

I had a moment of theological panic. I had been told on a number of occasions in Asian contexts that the honoring of ancestors was an urgent consideration for many recent converts, but I had simply filed it away as an interesting topic to think about sometime. But here the issue was urged upon me with desperate pleading. Melissa was not asking for a theological disquisition—she wanted words to use when she returned home to talk to her Buddhist parents.

What came immediately to mind was the Hubbard talk, so I told her about Jesus's encounter with the friends of the paralyzed man. Jesus was making it clear to them that he honors the faith that we show on behalf of others who may be incapable of having their own faith at that point. It could be, I told her, that the Lord was allowing her faith to count in his dealings with her ancestors. At the very least, I told her, she could tell her parents that she honors her ancestors so much that she fervently prays that the Lord will look upon them with his divine favor.

While Melissa responded with obvious gratitude, I knew that I was winging it a bit theologically. I was thankful, though, that she had pushed me to think about the subject, and I have continued since then to wrestle with her question. I am convinced that what I had said had some biblical basis, and even if I had gone too far theologically—which, again, I was not convinced was the case—I at least compensated for the theological insensitivities of Christians who have in the past dismissed her kind of concern as a temptation to compromise with "paganism."

Connecting with Ancestors

One theologian who has given me some confidence in what I told Melissa is Simon Chan, a Pentecostal scholar who teaches in Singapore. In his book focusing on "grassroots" Christianity in Asia, Chan argues that Western theologians frequently are ignorant of the spiritual challenges that shape the thought and practice of local Christian communities in Asia, particularly those posed by the honor-and-shame culture that is prominent there. We evangelicals in the West typically concentrate on the concepts of sin and guilt, and while Chan does not deny the fact of our guilty sinful condition, he argues that to fail also to pay attention to honor-and-shame themes is to miss much of what the Bible tells us about our shared humanity.

Chan addresses the topic of the veneration of ancestors, pointing to the same concerns that were raised so earnestly by my young Chinese translator. Local church leaders in Asian settings, Chan reports, are aware of the ways that many missionaries ignored these realities, and Pentecostal movements have now been giving serious attention to ways of remedying this inattention. They have expanded the theological concept of the *communio sanctorum* to focus on continuing relationships between the living and the dead. Furthermore, these movements have instituted "elaborate rituals relating to evangelizing of and communion with the dead," including a "commending of the dead to the mercy of God."[2] Chan cautiously approves of these explorations, saying they are "Christologically grounded" and "sufficiently distinguished from Confucian and Taoist ancestral rites." Furthermore, he says, "when bold steps are taken to find appropriate Christian ritual expressions of ancestral veneration, fresh theological insights have emerged."[3]

Chan rightly stresses the importance of these explorations, noting that the deep commitment to "ancestor veneration underscores the unsurpassed value placed on the family in Asia."[4] Given my own Kuyperian embrace of the idea of "sphere sovereignty," I take Chan's counsel with utmost seriousness. We Reformed types must attend more carefully than we have in the past to how the sphere of family life takes different shapes in diverse cultural contexts. Doing sensitive theological work on these matters is an obligation that we have to those who have come to a saving knowledge of Jesus Christ in contexts where ancestral veneration is so deeply embedded in their patterns of configuring created life. And, I should add, we owe it also to our own Western Christian communities, where many profound—and disturbing!— new challenges have been raised in recent decades about traditional assumptions about family and marriage.

I would like to know more about those "Christian ritual expressions of ancestral veneration." Since they focus, in Chan's

2. Simon Chan, *Grassroots Asian Theology: Thinking the Faith from the Ground Up* (Downers Grove, IL: IVP Academic, 2014), 193–94.

3. Chan, *Grassroots Asian Theology*, 202.

4. Chan, *Grassroots Asian Theology*, 189.

words, on "evangelizing of and communion with the dead," they seem to be seen as more than mere Christian-flavored séances. Nor are the Asian Christians simply sponsoring prayer meetings in which the names of the unevangelized are mentioned. In these current practices, the Christian community is doing some *mediatorial*-type work liturgically. Or, to use a term in its rather technical sense, they are engaging in an important *representational* task.

I take the idea of representation here from Suzanne McDonald's intriguing and insightful 2010 study of election, where she highlights the dual role of God's elect people of representing *God to the world* as well as *the world to God*. This twofold representational calling, McDonald argues, is central "for understanding the nature and purpose of election."[5] McDonald offers a rich and nuanced discussion of various dimensions of the Calvinist doctrine of election. Her detailed study has not only reinforced my own appreciation of the doctrine of election, but it has expanded and even corrected my grasp of that doctrine in significant ways—including in the implications for my discussion here of salvific generosity. After I give a brief account of McDonald's overall project, I will show how her views on election cast light on the issues I have been exploring thus far.

A Common Quest

McDonald lets us know at the beginning of her exploration that her desire to get clear about the doctrine of election is a "deeply personal" one that begins with her firm endorsement

5. Suzanne McDonald, *Re-imaging Election: Divine Election as Representing God to Others and Others to God* (Grand Rapids: Eerdmans, 2010), xiv.

of "the theological contours that shape a Reformed approach to election." These "contours" that stand out for her are: that our salvation is made possible only by "God's sovereign grace, unconditioned and unmerited"; that in election "God chooses some and not others"; and that in our human responses to divine grace, "there is no capacity to love, trust and follow God that God does not give."[6]

McDonald focuses at length on two major Reformed figures: the seventeenth-century Puritan John Owen and the great Karl Barth. I am glad that she chose these two. I have regularly admired Owen from a distance, and her study has brought his wise theological insights closer to my mind. And McDonald's careful attention to the nuances of Karl Barth's thought has helped me to take his thought more seriously than I have in the past. In my own embrace and development of neo-Calvinist ideas, I have often dropped critical comments about Barthian thought, suggesting, for example, that his Christocentric theology bordered on Christo-monism, and that he seriously lacked a robust doctrine of creation. When I have touched on Barthian thought in my classes on theology of culture, I have required my students to read his debates with Emil Brunner on general revelation, siding strongly with Brunner's interpretations of the Pauline writings and the views of John Calvin.

While I still hold to my main criticisms of Barth on those matters, McDonald has shown me how to engage his thought with the care he deserves. I have been especially taken with the way she shows how Barth in his early writings—his Göttingen lectures in the mid-1920s—sees predestination as "emphatically individual, unconditional and double in accordance with the strictest Reformed orthodoxy. He upholds the Synod of Dordt

6. McDonald, *Re-imaging Election*, xiii–xiv.

as containing all that needs to be said concerning God's relationship to humanity and ours to God." The common ground between Owen and the early Barth on these basic themes means, McDonald observes, that they "are substantially at one in their understanding of the contours of God's election."[7]

In his subsequent writings about election, however, Barth moved in a different direction. In the second volume of his *Church Dogmatics*, he placed a strong emphasis on the idea that, as McDonald puts it, "in Jesus Christ—and in him alone—we see the electing God and the elect man. . . . Jesus Christ is not only the one elect, but also, for Barth, the only truly elected human being."[8] This led Barth to a broader understanding of what it means to be "in Christ." Since all human beings are seen as represented by Christ's status as *the* elect human being, all human beings are beneficiaries of God's electing grace.

McDonald points out that the key element in Barth's shift was his abandonment of the strong pneumatological element that has been seen as fundamental to the orthodox Reformed view of election. For classical Calvinism, to be "in Christ" is inextricably linked to being regenerated by the work of the Holy Spirit, and evidence of regeneration takes the form of, among other things, a genuine sense of one's sinfulness and a full reliance on the gift of sovereign grace for the redeemed life. On the later Barthian view, though, persons can be considered to be "in Christ" without ever exhibiting any signs of coming to saving faith. McDonald acknowledges that this is biblically unacceptable. We cannot "speak of being 'in Christ' in ways that

7. McDonald, *Re-imaging Election*, 35–36.

8. McDonald, *Re-imaging Election*, 43. Her account of Barth's shift in his thinking here refers to his *Church Dogmatics* II/2 (Edinburgh: T&T Clark, 1957), 161–62, 318–19, 346, 352–53.

suggest this can be considered (and achieved) apart from the Spirit's work in us."[9]

While McDonald sides with Owen's "rich and powerfully integrated understanding of the Spirit's role in election,"[10] she does credit the later Barth with rightly emphasizing our calling as believers to nurture a sense of solidarity with the larger human community. She is especially taken with Barth's portrayal of "the relational dynamic of the Trinitarian being of God *ad intra*"—that is, the mutual loving relationship that binds together the Father, Son, and Spirit. But the Trinity also has an *ad extra* character. It directs itself beyond its internal life. The triune God, says Barth, "is also God-for-the-other, God-for-us."[11]

As the unique revelation of the life and character of the divine Trinity, then, Christ shows us "that to image the relational God is not and cannot be solely an end in itself." This applies to our elect status. McDonald observes that an individual who has received saving grace through the ministry of the Holy Spirit is also called to direct his or her life toward the "other" by being incorporated into the life of the Christian community. But this community in turn is called to be directed beyond ourselves toward that portion of humanity who are not in "communion with God."[12] McDonald sees this outward facing of the redeemed people as bearing witness to the fact that there is an *ad extra* dimension that is essential to the very purpose of election.

The *ad intra* of the ecclesial community's fellowship, however, is also intimately linked to the *ad extra* of our relationship with the "other" of the larger human community, as well as to the whole creation. And here McDonald endorses Barth's insis-

9. McDonald, *Re-imaging Election*, 69.
10. McDonald, *Re-imaging Election*, 29.
11. McDonald, *Re-imaging Election*, 125.
12. McDonald, *Re-imaging Election*, 127, 131.

tence that our Christian for-the-other relationship with those who have not accepted the promises of the gospel must be one of solidarity. However, she does not follow Barth in seeing this solidarity as consisting in our sharing with them an ontological status of being "in Christ." As we have seen, she firmly rejects the idea that people can have that status apart from the regenerating work of the Spirit.

Of course, that the elect community has a "for others" mandate from God has never been seriously questioned in the Christian tradition. That Jesus himself told his immediate followers, before his ascension to heaven, that they were to "go and make disciples of all nations" (Matt. 28:19) is impossible to ignore. This evangelistic task is certainly important for the representational function that McDonald sees as central to God's electing purposes. But the scope of the representational calling is much broader. As Owen put it, Christians do not serve the purpose of election when "they do very little [to] either represent or glorify God in the world." Rather, as those who have been elected to a process of growing into the image of Jesus Christ, believers are called in their relations with "all mankind" to "labor after conformity unto God, *and to express our likeness unto him*."[13]

"Blessing" the World

In the opening pages of my second chapter, I highlighted the importance of taking a step beyond the passive character of the

13. McDonald, *Re-imaging Election*, 25. She is citing Owen's argument in his *Pneumatologia; or, A Discourse concerning the Holy Spirit*, in *The Works of John Owen*, ed. William H. Gould, 24 vols. (London: Johnstone & Hunter, 1850–1855), 3:587–88, also 582–84.

Calvinist understanding of election. God has *acted upon* us with sovereign grace, doing for us what we could not bring about by our own efforts. But, I observed, the next question has to be: What does God elect us *for*? What does God's electing grace empower us to *do* as agents of his kingdom?

Using McDonald's terminology, I was pointing to our assignment as elect people to represent God *to* the world. My typical way of putting this point has been that we are called as a covenant community to "show forth" what it means to demonstrate communal conformity to God's creating and redeeming purposes.

McDonald's helpful discussion of what it means for the elect to "bless" the creation made me aware of the need to be clearer in my own formulations on this matter. She rightly argues that our *ad extra* relationship with the larger human community requires more than simply "showing" what it means to live communally in obedience to God's will. She makes her case, in good Reformed fashion, by insisting that God's purposes in electing the New Testament church are continuous with his purposes in the election of ancient Israel. Furthermore, she observes, God elected the people of Israel so that they could be the means of fulfilling God's promise to Abraham, that "in you all the families of the earth shall be blessed" (Gen. 12:3 NRSV)—a promise that she sees as central now to the election of the New Testament church.[14]

In discussing this mandate to "bless" the nations, she interacts critically with the views of several contemporary theologians. She finds Christopher Seitz, for example, suggesting that Israel could perform its "blessing" assignment "simply by living

14. McDonald, *Re-imaging Election*, 94–116, where McDonald makes her case by drawing on insights from Christopher Seitz and N. T. Wright.

out its covenanted life before God."[15] And she finds a similar emphasis in Walter Brueggemann, who posits that Israel's representation to the larger human community is facilitated, as she puts it, "simply by being Israel in the utter particularity of its covenant relationship with God." On this kind of understanding of Israel's mission, she observes, Israel does not even need to be aware of what it is doing. It is faithful to its elect status just by showing in its life together what it means for a nation to be in a faithful covenant relation with God.[16]

My own ways of describing our divine calling to represent God to the unbelieving world have typically been similar to the ones McDonald finds in Seitz and Brueggemann—a portrayal that I now see as a kind of "show and tell" perspective. And that is certainly part of the picture. By our communal existence we, as God's elect people, "show forth" what it means to be faithful to God's purposes for collective human life. We are also called to "tell," to look for opportunities to explain the patterns of our lives while also inviting others to join us in our communal obedience.

My actual thinking on this subject, though, has been closer to McDonald's more robust "blessing" perspective than would appear from my frequent use of "show and tell" language. This is clear, for example, in the position I have taken in an ongoing division within the neo-Calvinist movement regarding the necessity of extra-ecclesial organizations devoted to thought and action within specific cultural "spheres": Christians in the arts, in farming, in politics, and the like. In his book *Dutch Calvinism*

15. McDonald, *Re-imaging Election*, 97. She is citing Christopher Seitz, *Figured Out: Typology and Providence in Christian Scripture* (Louisville: Westminster John Knox, 2001), 151.

16. McDonald, *Re-imaging Election*, 99. She is following here Brueggemann's argument in his *Theology of the Old Testament: Testimony, Dispute, Advocacy* (Minneapolis: Fortress, 1991), 413.

in Modern America, James Bratt distinguishes between two quite different ways that the followers of Abraham Kuyper have seen the point of those organizations. Bratt labels the positions "positive Calvinist" and "antitheticalists." The antitheticalists view these groups as a necessary way of reinforcing a sense of separating from "worldly" patterns of cultural engagement, while the positive Kuyperians see participating in these organizations as a training ground and platform for productive engagement with the larger culture.[17]

Those of us who emphasize the reality of common grace as a nonsalvific divine favor toward the behavior and thought of unregenerate people use this doctrine to argue for an active learning from and cooperation with those who do not share our faith commitments. McDonald has helped me to see, however, that when we "positive Kuyperians" express our common grace perspective, we typically emphasize the need for believers to be open to receiving gifts from the unbelieving world: truths that they can teach us and manifestations of goodness and beauty in what they make available to us. Thus, common grace is typically presented as acknowledging how the unbelieving world blesses *us*.

Obviously, that is a good thing to preach, given the "us versus them" posture that often characterizes Christian attitudes toward the larger culture. Not only should that use of common grace not be seen as problematic from McDonald's perspective, but the acknowledgment of receiving blessings *from* the world can be linked intimately to our taking with utmost seriousness the task of representing the world *to* God. That task of representing the world *to* God is important to my overall discussion in this book.

17. James Bratt, *Dutch Calvinism in Modern America* (Grand Rapids: Eerdmans, 1984), 50.

Advocating for the "Other"

In her comments criticizing Brueggemann's depiction of Israel's communal calling, McDonald does credit him with hinting at an important insight in a comment he makes about "Israel's designation as a 'kingdom of priests' in Exodus 19:5–6." She explains, "Brueggemann remarks that while this does primarily signify that Israel exists to point to Yahweh, there is also the tantalizing possibility that 'perhaps this nation is offered as a priest for other nations of the world. . . . And finally . . . to make communion between Yahweh and the world possible.'"[18]

In our "priestly" role as the elect people, we represent the needs and concerns of the world before God. This "holding of the other in the self before God" is, McDonald says, "intrinsic to the very being of the elect community." But the fact that we as persons "in Christ" are doing this "holding" does not mean that those "held" by us thereby share in our "in Christ" status. McDonald is consistently clear that "*the believing community and the believing community alone can be described as elect in Christ.*"[19] But—and this is crucial to her case—since believers have come to be "in Christ" by the regenerating work of the Holy Spirit, when we are holding the unbelieving others in our own redeemed selfhood, we are representing them in a special way in God's presence (140–42, also 131). Just as "through Israel the promises of God were to reach beyond the covenant people to the nations, so it is because there is a community of the new covenant—a people united to Christ by the Spirit, and so participating already in the salvation which has been wrought by

18. McDonald, *Re-imaging Election*, 100. She is citing Brueggemann, *Theology of the Old Testament*, 430, 433.

19. McDonald, *Re-imaging Election*, 114. Hereafter, page references from this work will be given in parentheses in the text.

God in him—that those who are as yet outside that community are also held provisionally within the sphere of God's promised blessings" (152).

Some obvious questions come to mind at this point. What is the *content* of this representational task? What actually goes *into* our bringing non-Christians into this "promised blessings" sphere? What are we asking God to *do* with those whom we have come to hold within our own selves in our presence before the Lord? What do we anticipate will be the *results* of our representational efforts?

While McDonald does not give us much detail about these matters, she does assure us that she "strongly upholds the exclusivity of the concept of election, insisting with Owen and the historic Reformed tradition—and contra Barth—that to speak of the elect is to refer, after the resurrection of Christ, only to those who are united to Christ by the Spirit through faith" (187). This means that "now and at the eschaton, only those upon whom the Spirit is bestowed to this effect are united to Christ and so drawn into the dynamic of the triune life, and [that] this work of the Spirit is entirely the free, unconditioned, gracious gift of God" (192).

In expounding upon this, however, she does make much of the "relational" nature of human personhood, a theme she employs creatively in her understanding of what it means for believers to "hold" unbelievers within their own selves, as a means of expediting the divine "blessings" to humankind as such. Here she offers a profound "parable," looking at how those whose loved ones have moved into extreme dementia can "hold" the personhood of those loved ones within their own personhood when the loved ones themselves are no longer aware of being distinct selves. She is clear, of course, on the limits of the parable's applicability, but her exploration of how the parable does illuminate aspects of the "holding" relationship is nonetheless compelling.

On what all of this means for the final scope of God's salvific mercies, McDonald wisely refrains from affirming universal salvation. The possibility that some human beings may ultimately be rejected by God, she acknowledges, "remains an incomprehensible mystery which is not to be resolved"—although she does allow that her representational account might at least allow for "the possibility of a hope for all that is pneumatologically shaped as well as christologically grounded" (193–94). What she *is* confident of, however, in setting forth her account of "the pneumatological dynamic of election to representation is that the being and doing of the elect new covenant community, as it lives out its calling and grows into the image of God, lies at the heart of God's purposes for the countless multitudes of every tribe and tongue who will come to find their true eschatological identity and personhood in Christ by the Spirit" (194).

9

Salvific Intensifications

SINCE WARFIELD AND HIS COLLEAGUES, and now Suzanne McDonald, have argued convincingly that the salvation of a vast number of human beings is not unthinkable from a Calvinist perspective, how might we imagine specific cases of adults coming to true faith even with no opportunity to hear the gospel proclaimed? Actually, as we saw, Shedd does offer a hypothetical case. A person in an unevangelized region experiences a deep sorrow for his corrupt deeds and thoughts and senses the need to rely for forgiveness and correction on something beyond himself. He pleads for mercy in his heart and begins to lead a life marked by gratitude for the spiritual resources that have entered his life. On Shedd's characterization of this case, the man is showing the fruits of election, which means that the Spirit has planted the seed of redemption in his soul. The man does not know who his Savior is, but, says Shedd, the man *would* acknowledge Jesus as the guarantor of his salvation if he *were* to hear the gospel message. Nor does Shedd seem to think that this kind of case is extremely rare. We have to posit relatively frequent similar stories if we are to sustain our conviction that "the vast majority" of humankind will be saved in the end.

But what about the cases closer to home? What about those persons who live in evangelized cultures who for a variety of reasons seem—humanly speaking, of course—incapable of seriously considering Christ's claims? Here I want to linger a bit on the Muslim woman who was raped and whose child was killed by "Christian" soldiers. She seems destined to go through her life nurturing a deep hostility to anything associated with Christianity. But we do need to attend to the important factor that I earlier mentioned in passing. Her child, having died in infancy, is in heaven with Jesus. She is in fact the mother of an elect human being. Could something like the unbelieving husband of 1 Corinthians 7:14—he is "made holy" by his wife's faith—apply to the Muslim mother as well? Indeed, could it be that her child, now in heaven, holds her as his own person, representing her *to God*? And might we also draw parallels to the continuing prayers of Dennis's mother for her son, for the heartfelt gratitude of Sarah's friends for what AA meetings have meant in her life, and for the assurances that Melissa gives to her Buddhist parents about the status of her ancestors in God's eyes?

All of that is, to be sure, a matter of theological speculation. But the speculation has urgent implications for how we Christians think about the eternal destinies of people we love. Furthermore, something like these theological imaginings are necessary to put spiritual flesh on the important ideas of Warfield and his friends. We need to find very practical ways for holding in our own persons the hopes and fears of unbelievers. This includes, I am convinced, exploring very seriously what it would look like to give faithful Calvinist form and content to the kinds of liturgies that Simon Chan tells us have been developed in Asian Pentecostal contexts.

Pentecost Completed

My reference to things Pentecostal leads in to what I want to emphasize at the conclusion of my exploration of Calvinist salvific generosity. What all of this comes down to for me is the central emphasis on the working of the Holy Spirit. The article in the Westminster Confession that was the reference point in the Presbyterian debates of the 1890s was about the ways in which the Holy Spirit brings people to Christ, and the orthodox Calvinists made their case with an uncompromising emphasis on salvation by sovereign grace alone through the atoning work of Jesus Christ. W. G. T. Shedd, for one, had no use for depicting small children as not-yet-guilty sinners. We saw him arguing that "though the infant has committed no acts of known and wilful transgression, yet his heart is estranged from God, and his will is at enmity with the holy law of God." We also saw A. A. Hodge refusing the notion that children constitute a special class of humans who are granted a generic salvific upgrade. While all dying infants are elected, he argued, each one individually must be "regenerated and sanctified immediately by God without the use of means."

This strict focus on the central role of the Holy Spirit in salvation was also emphasized by Suzanne McDonald in her critique of Karl Barth, who in his later theology shifted away from the classic Calvinist insistence that being "in Christ" requires the regenerating work of the Holy Spirit. Barth had come to see what it means for individuals to be thought of as "in Christ" without the presence in their lives of the signs of regeneration. McDonald finds this unacceptable. No one, she says, will inherit the eternal kingdom without experiencing the individual regenerating work of the Holy Spirit. She even uses italics to convey that conviction: "*The believing commu-*

nity and the believing community alone can be described as elect in Christ."[1]

It is precisely because McDonald stands firm in that conviction that she can direct our attention to larger mysteries we can anticipate in the promise about the "last days" proclaimed at Pentecost.

> What we see in the extraordinary outpouring of the Spirit upon the apostles at Pentecost re-presents the partial, proleptic fulfilment of this promise. The final outpouring of the Spirit upon all flesh is still to come. . . . When this full and final outpouring takes place, we may assume that the outcome will be consistent with what we have come to know of the Spirit's person and work in the present. . . . We must assume that at the parousia it will likewise be by the Spirit alone that any of us will confess Christ as Lord, be drawn into the fullness of communion of the Triune God and with one another in him, and come as a result to the fullest realization of our true personhood.[2]

Two things should be obvious in what McDonald and other Calvinists highlight about the relationship of the Spirit's work in the present age and the completed outpouring that is yet to come in the eschaton. One is that there is a continuity between the present and the glorified future. One theme about the present work of the Spirit often highlighted in Reformed theology is the dynamic work of the Spirit in the larger creation. Here is a strong affirmation on that from Kuyper: "The work of the

1. Suzanne McDonald, *Re-imaging Election: Divine Election as Representing God to Others and Others to God* (Grand Rapids: Eerdmans, 2010), 114.

2. McDonald, *Re-imaging Election*, 170–71.

Holy Spirit consists in leading all creation to *its destiny*, the final purpose of which is the glory of God."[3] Bavinck also stresses the dynamic element in discussing the status of non-Christian religions. The past Christian view of the founders of other religions simply as "enemies of God, accomplices of the devil" is not feasible, he says, in the light of "both history and psychology." Then he offers this theological verdict, featuring a dynamic depiction of the presence of the Holy Spirit in non-Christian religious contexts: "Also among pagans, says Scripture, there is a revelation of God, an illumination by the Logos, a working of God's Spirit."[4] Bavinck here is echoing John Calvin himself on this subject, when the Reformer, in observing that because there is an "admirable light of truth shining" in the thoughts of pagan thinkers, said we "dishonor the Spirit of God"[5] if we refuse to accept the truths that they have to offer us. Nor does the dynamism of the Spirit cease in the eschaton. On the contrary, as Geerhardus Vos expounds at length in his study of Pauline eschatology, the proper "arena" of the Holy Spirit is the future age of the new creation.[6] It seems appropriate to assume, then, that in making our formulations regarding what will characterize the completed Pentecostal outpouring in the eschaton, we must be careful not to dishonor the Spirit, who will continue

3. Abraham Kuyper, *The Work of the Holy Spirit*, trans. Henri de Vries (New York: Funk & Wagnalls, 1900), 22.

4. Herman Bavinck, *Reformed Dogmatics*, vol. 1, *Prologomenon*, ed. John Bolt, trans. John Vriend (Grand Rapids: Baker Academic, 2004), 318.

5. John Calvin, *Institutes of the Christian Religion*, ed. John T. McNeill, trans. Ford Lewis Battles, Library of Christian Classics, vols. 20 and 21 (Philadelphia: Westminster, 1960), 2.3.6, p. 273.

6. Geerhardus Vos, "The Eschatological Aspect of the Pauline Conception of the Holy Spirit," in *Biblical and Theological Studies*, by the Members of the Faculty of Princeton Theological Seminary (New York: Charles Scribner's Sons, 1912), 209–59.

to be, at the end of history as we know it, the One who works "when, and where, and how he pleaseth."

Accents and Intensifications

In chapter 3, I discussed Gijsbert van den Brink's helpful discussion of various theological "stances," with their respective "accents" and "intensifications." In applying that to Reformed theology, I said I had initially found Kosuke Koyama's discussion of "stingy" views of God helpful, only to decide later that it was unfair to apply that label to Calvinists who have a more restrictive view than I hold on the scope of the positive working of the Holy Spirit in human hearts. It is important to acknowledge that Warfield and his colleagues did have critics on the subject from within the Calvinist theological community, critics who spoke with the same accent as Warfield, the Hodges, and Shedd, but who insisted on different intensifications.

As I already acknowledged with reference to Herman Hoeksema and his associates, I recognize that theological accent in my own deep places. Even more, I also am deeply familiar with the intensification that would characterize their rejection of the 1905 statement on the Westminster Confession. They would see the Presbyterians as issuing clear verdicts on matters that are better left in the realm of divine mysteries. There have been many occasions where, in explaining and defending Calvinist teachings, I have said that a specific theological concern should be left to the hidden counsel of God. I have learned that intensification in our Calvinist ways of speaking about the divine mysteries from the same confessions that Herman Hoeksema loved, and on many occasions I have heeded confessional voices that have reminded me with the Calvinist accent not to stray far beyond the clear teachings of Scripture. Here is one warning that I have learned to heed, from the Belgic Confession on divine providence: "And as to what [God] doth surpassing human understanding we will not curiously inquire into it further than our capacity will admit of; but with the greatest humility and reverence adore the righteous judgments of God which are hid from us, contenting ourselves that we are disciples of Christ, to learn only those things which he has revealed to us in his Word without transgressing these limits."[7] And here is another instance, where the Canons of Dort discuss how we properly gain the assurance of our election: "The elect in due time, though in various degrees and in different measures, attain the assurance of this their eternal and unchangeable election, not by inquisitively prying into the secret and deep things of God, but by observing in themselves, with a spiritual joy and holy pleasure, the infallible fruits of election pointed out in the Word of God."[8]

What is significant about each of these confessional warnings is the insistence that we must not go beyond what God "has revealed to us in his Word" (Belgic), or beyond what is "pointed out in the Word of God" (Canons). The question, then, that must be addressed by Calvinists on the salvific status of a deceased child from a non-Christian family is whether believing that the child is saved takes us beyond the teachings of the Word. To speak clearly about the eternal destiny of dying children is not misguided speculation.

Imagine a Calvinist pastor visiting a couple who, while not church members, had until recently been attending his services.

7. Belgic Confession, article 13, in *The Creeds of Christendom, with a History and Critical Notes*, ed. Philip Schaff, vol. 3 (Grand Rapids: Baker Books, 1996), 397.

8. Canons of the Synod of Dort, First Head of Doctrine, article 12, in Schaff, *The Creeds of Christendom*, 3:583–84.

He had heard that their newborn infant has just died, and he wanted to reach out to them in their grief. When he arrives at their home, they are obviously reluctant to talk with him. They tell him that while they have benefited from his ministry, they had looked into the history of Calvinism, and they decided that they could not identify with the Reformed tradition. And now—given the terrible loss of their child—they feel justified in that decision. "How could we join a church that teaches about a God who sends unbaptized babies to hell?" the wife asks.

Would the pastor be misleading them theologically if he tells them that he is firmly convinced that their daughter is now in the eternal embrace of Jesus? I am convinced that the pastor can speak in confidence to them about God's love for their child. And I have drawn assurance in that confidence from the ways that the Hodges, Warfield, and Shedd have addressed the subject.

To repeat: I understand the accent of those who think it is wrong to have this kind of assurance. God's sovereign ways are indeed far beyond our ability to comprehend, and it is simply good Calvinism to acknowledge the dangers of (quoting Belgic) "inquisitively prying into the secret and deep things of God." However, the confessional Calvinists who have boldly proclaimed a salvific generosity were themselves intensifying important Calvinist convictions. Throughout his Word, God has in countless ways revealed his character to us, which means that we can be assured by what he has shown us about his purposes, that he will not abandon his announced goals for the creation that he loves.

10

The Great Gathering

HOWEVER THE NINETEENTH-CENTURY Princetonians would explain the theological support for their large-number vision of the end time, it would certainly not comport with Darryl Hart's commendation of these theologians for not having contributed any significant new ideas to the body of traditional Calvinist teaching. Hart's insistence that his Princeton heroes were willing to be "boring or predictable" in "preserving the content and character of Reformed orthodoxy" is difficult to defend in the light of the accounts I have given here. The Princeton scholars clearly shared the assessment of their friend Shedd, that the Westminster Confession is a "sufficiently broad and liberal creed"—not, he explained, "sufficiently broad and liberal for every man and every denomination; but it is as broad and liberal for a Calvinist as any Calvinist should desire."[1] Furthermore, they were committed to actively presenting a Calvinism that showed a more generous spirit than had often characterized the Calvinism of the past.

1. William G. T. Shedd, *Calvinism Pure and Mixed: A Defence of the Westminster Standards* (Carlisle, PA: Banner of Truth Trust, 1986), 6.

Nor was that generous theological spirit ignored by theologians who otherwise were critical of the Princetonians' convictions. Earlier we saw Schaff criticizing the historical claims made by Warfield and others regarding the intentions of the seventeenth-century Westminster divines. And that was not the only time Schaff had crossed theological swords with Princeton scholars. As a prominent proponent of the Mercersburg Theology—a school of Reformed thought with a strong sacramental character—Schaff had engaged in published exchanges with Charles Hodge on a number of topics.[2] But in the debates about the election of infants, Schaff tempered his criticisms of the Princeton folks by observing that their advocacy of the inclusivist view, even if based on faulty historical grounds, was "a progress in the right direction."[3] And he singled out for special praise "the fathers and founders of the Princeton theology," Archibald Alexander and Charles Hodge, "for what they accomplished by liberalizing the Calvinistic theology." They had spoken out "against uncharitable anti-popery fanaticism," affirming "the Church character of the Roman Catholic communion, and the validity of her baptism," and in the debates over revision they had "taught the salvation of *all* infants dying in infancy."[4] And about Charles Hodge in particular, Schaff wrote warmly of "the goodness of his heart and his amiable temper [that] gave to his whole theology a sweet, evangelical, and catholic one, which favorably contrasts with the severity and narrowness of older systems."[5]

---

2. Schaff's theological exchanges with Charles Hodge are chronicled in James Hastings Nichols, *The Mercersburg Theology* (Oxford: Oxford University Press, 1966).

3. Philip Schaff, *Creed Revision in the Presbyterian Churches* (New York: Charles Scribner's Sons, 1890), 20.

4. Schaff, *Creed Revision*, 49.

5. Schaff, *Creed Revision*, 50.

It should be clear by now that at the heart of the orthodox Calvinists' shared theological project was their desire to bear witness to divine generosity. W. G. T. Shedd stated the aims of the project clearly when he wrote about the need to counter the depiction of the Calvinist God "as a tyrannical sovereign who is destitute of love and mercy for any but an elect few, . . . a Being who creates some men in order to damn them."[6] This picture of the Calvinist God that Shedd rejects is the same one that I set out to counter in this book, and his depiction serves as a kind of checklist for reviewing what I have come up with.

We need to explicitly state that a nonuniversalist Calvinism cannot avoid the charge that God favors some and not others. In my popular-level book on Calvinism, I related a brief conversation I had on the subject with a Jewish couple.[7] A rabbi friend had invited me to speak to a Jewish audience about the Ten Commandments. I began my talk by explaining how my Calvinist tradition adheres to a "divine command" ethical perspective. Afterward a Jewish couple came up to thank me for my talk. But, they said, they were puzzled that I had identified myself as a Calvinist. "You seem like a nice person," the woman said. "That's not the image we have of Calvinists." Then her husband quickly added: "Yes—like, don't Calvinists believe that God elects certain people and not others? That seems to me to be a horrible belief!"

I smiled and asked them: "Don't you Jewish folks believe that God chooses some and not others? In ancient times the Lord chose Israel as his special people, and not the Amalekites or the Philistines." They took my point in a good spirit.

---

6. Shedd, *Calvinism Pure and Mixed*, 15.

7. Richard J. Mouw, *Calvinism in the Las Vegas Airport: Making Connections in Today's World* (Grand Rapids: Zondervan, 2004), 31–32.

They hadn't thought of that, they said. "That certainly gives us something to think about!" It is also something to think about for Christians who are offended that God shows more favor to some individuals than to others but have no problem with God's being selective in his decision in ancient times to dispense his covenantal blessings on a specific *people*.

We have set forth here, though, reasons why Calvinism need not understand God's saving mercies as dispensed only to "an elect *few*." Certainly for Shedd and his Princeton friends, a proper understanding of the debated article in the Westminster Confession encourages us to see the Holy Spirit as even regenerating people who do not have access to the proclaimed Word.

And what about the Calvinist God "as a tyrannical sovereign who is destitute of love and mercy"? The salvation of all dying infants by sovereign grace certainly serves as counterevidence to this charge. But we can add more. As we saw in discussing how God goes about saving infants, some theologians see infant salvation as a kind of "class action" operation. They argue that because children before "the age of accountability" are not yet to be seen by God as responsible for acting out of their sinful natures, those who die in their childhood are automatically beneficiaries of saving grace. Not so in the Calvinist scheme. The nineteenth-century Calvinists whom we have been discussing refused to create a special category for children. The only salvific hope for any human being, young or old, is an individual act of divine grace. As the Westminster article makes clear, infants are saved in the same manner as the subgroup of *adults* who are regenerated by the Spirit apart from the proclamation of the Word.

Consider, in the light of these distinctions, the Muslim child killed by "Christian" soldiers. On the "class action" view, there is no special outpouring of "love and mercy" toward *that child*. The infant may not yet have done anything to offend the Lord, but for Shedd and his Princeton colleagues, the baby is already seen as a sinful being. As a dying infant, however, God lovingly chooses to show sovereign mercy to that child.

The insistence here on the individualized character of the Holy Spirit's work of regeneration is underscored by the Canons of Dort's description of how a person is brought to saving faith: "This grace of generation does not treat men as senseless stocks and blocks, nor take away their will and its properties, neither does violence thereto, but spiritually quickens, heals, corrects, and at the same time sweetly and powerfully bends it ... [toward] a ready and sincere spiritual obedience."[8] The Spirit not only respects the dignity of the sinner's will by committing no violence against it, but the Spirit bends the will "sweetly and powerfully" toward repentance and obedience.

"Sweet" Grace

The Canons' "sweetly" image leads me to return to my second chapter and the example of Jonathan Edwards. His "Sinners in the Hands of an Angry God" sermon as a written document is marvelously crafted. Nor is it confused theologically. But I would not commend it to a person looking for a piece of writing that would give a good sense of Calvinist teaching.

I was pleased to discover that Edwards gives us a different picture in his "Personal Narrative."[9] The spiritual struggles that

8. Canons of Dort, Third and Fourth Main Points of Doctrine, article 16, in *The Creeds of Christendom, with a History and Critical Notes*, ed. Philip Schaff, vol. 3 (Grand Rapids: Baker Books, 1996), 591.

9. Jonathan Edwards, "Personal Narrative," pdf downloaded from online

plagued him in his youth resemble the depiction of the divine character in his "Sinners in the Hands" sermon. He nurtured objections to "the doctrine of God's sovereignty, in choosing whom he would to eternal life, and rejecting whom he pleased; leaving them to perish, and be everlastingly tormented in hell. It used to appear like a horrible doctrine to me."

There came a time, though, when, he said, "I seemed to be convinced, and fully satisfied, as to this sovereignty of God, and his justice in thus eternally disposing of men, according to his sovereign pleasure." While he was rationally convinced of this theological system, he was not able to sense "any extraordinary influence of God's Spirit in it."

Eventually, though, he did come to experience this theology of grace in a new way while reading the Canticles (Song of Solomon). As he meditated on the references to "the rose of Sharon" and "the lily of the valleys," they came "sweetly to represent, the loveliness and beauty of Jesus Christ." This brought to him "an inward sweetness," along with "a calm, sweet abstraction from all the concerns of this world." Edwards continues with at least two dozen more "sweetness" references. One more example, with the references italicized by me: "I walked abroad alone, in a solitary place in my father's pasture, for contemplation. And as I was walking there, and looking upon the sky and clouds, there came into my mind so *sweet* a sense of the glorious majesty and grace of God, as I know not how to express—I seemed to see them both in a *sweet* conjunction; majesty and meekness joined together: it was a *sweet*, and gentle, and holy majesty; and also a majestic meekness; an awful *sweetness*; a high, and great, and holy gentleness."

Jonathan Edwards Center at Yale University: http://edwards.yale.edu/ar chive/. All quotations here are from the first four pages.

In testifying to his profound sense of the sweetness of God's mercies, Edwards was giving evidence of his experience of the process described by the Canons: while doing no violence to the will of the individual, the Spirit "sweetly and powerfully bends" that will, bringing the person to a "ready and sincere spiritual obedience." Edwards did, of course, understand the company of the redeemed in small-number terms. When he joins Warfield and other Calvinists in the great multitude gathered in the heavenly courts, however, he will have even greater reason to celebrate "*how* sweet the sound" of the gospel of grace.

Divine Arbitrariness?

I must at least address the charge that God creates some human beings simply for the purpose of damning them. I have nothing to add to the kind of response to the depiction of Calvinist theology offered by Geerhardus Vos's nuanced account of divine love that I detailed in my first chapter.

Vos points out that while the Old Testament acknowledges a "divine love that reaches more widely than simply to the elect people," that wide-reaching love takes on a special focus in the New Testament writings, where the Savior's heart "was filled with tender compassion for every lost human soul, and was grieved even over those whose confirmed unbelief precluded all further hope of salvation." This compels us to hold, says Vos, that "there must be in God something corresponding to this."

We can certainly ask, of course, whether God's compassion for lost souls ends in eternity. We found Herman Bavinck refusing to say that it does. There are elements of divine mercy, he says, that even reach into hell. There is also N. T. Wright's argument that those who consistently act against God's will during their lifetimes go into eternity as monsters who have lost all of their humanness and are therefore beyond compassion. Those Calvinist speculations strike me as counting against the idea of divine arbitrariness.

Epilogue
Personal Concluding Thoughts

WHERE DO I END UP WITH ALL OF THIS? I have to admit that the perspective that I have been led to in my explorations in these pages is more than I set out to find. In chapter 2 I reported that in reading Herman Hoeksema I found myself opting for larger numbers when he began to move toward smaller ones, and I was eager to find Calvinist support for my impulse toward salvific generosity.

I have to admit that at the start I would have been content with a more modest perspective than what I discovered. My hope in setting out was that a serious study of Calvinist theologians whom I admired would show me that my generosity impulse was not a mere exercise in theological wishful thinking.

I had never before done any extensive scholarly work on Shedd and the nineteenth-century Princetonians, although I have on several occasions dipped into each of their writings. As I reported earlier, it was in investigating intra-Reformed debates about baptism that I came across the Presbyterian exchanges about confessional revision in the 1890s. I was pleasantly surprised that Warfield and Shedd enthusiastically endorsed the 1903 clarifying statement that all dying infants are beneficiaries of God's electing grace. I was even more impressed that they did not stop there but also commented favorably on the Westminster article's reference to "all others." And then there was more. I read Warfield's extensive critique of the "few there be" understanding of the number of the elect.

All of that would have been sufficient to satisfy my quest. I was not prepared, though, for Warfield's enthusiastic declaration for an expansive view that far exceeded what I had been hoping for: his affirmation that it will be revealed in the end time that the saving work of Christ "shall embrace the immensely greater part of the human race."[1] Nor does he offer this simply as his own verdict. It is, he wants us to see, a perspective that he shares with other Calvinist notables, as he makes clear by ending his essay with these affirmations:[2]

> "We have reason to believe," writes Charles Hodge, "that the number finally lost in comparison with the whole number of the saved will be very inconsiderable. Our blessed Lord, when surrounded by the innumerable company of the redeemed, will be hailed as the 'Salvator Hominum,' the Savior of men, as the Lamb that bore the sins of the world." Robert L. Dabney, expressing regret that the fact has been "too little pressed" "that ultimately the vast majority of the whole mass of humanity, including all generations, will be actually redeemed by Christ," adds, "There is to be a time, blessed by God, when literally all the then world will be saved by Christ, when the world will be finally, completely and wholly lifted by Christ out of the gulf, to sink no more. So there is a sense,

---

1. Benjamin Warfield, *Are They Few That Be Saved?* (New York: Our Hope Publications, 1918), 22.
2. Warfield, *Are They Few?*, 24.

most legitimate, in which Christ is the prospective Savior of the world." "Two errors, therefore," remarks W. G. T. Shedd, "are to be avoided: First, that all men are saved; secondly, that only a few men are saved. . . . Some . . . have represented the number of the reprobated as greater than that of the elect, or equal to it. They found this upon the word of Christ, 'Many are called, but few are chosen.' But this describes the situation at the time when our Lord spake, and not the result of His redemptive work. But when Christ shall have 'seen of the travail of His soul' and been 'satisfied' with what he has seen, when the whole course of the Gospel shall be complete, and shall be surveyed from beginning to end, it will be found that God's elect, or church, is 'a great multitude which no man can number, out of *all* nations, and kindreds, and peoples, and tongues,' and that their voice is as the voice of many waters, and as the voice of mighty thunderings, saying, 'Hallelujah, for the Lord God omnipotent reigneth.' Rev. 7:9, 19:6."

As many times as I have read these comments by the nineteenth-century Calvinist theologians, when I read them again I am still struck by the boldness of their affirmations of the large number of those who will be saved in the end. Even though Dabney, for example, tosses in a postmillennial projection about a mass conversion in a time that is yet to come in human history, he more than compensates for that questionable prediction with his declaration that the number of the elect will be comprised of "the vast majority of the whole mass of humanity, *including all generations*" (emphasis mine).

My Calvinist heroes, then, have given me more than I had hoped for. And in doing so they leave me with questions. What might Warfield, Shedd, and the Hodges have had in mind in giving substance to their grand vision? Of course, seeing all the dying children throughout history as having been elected to salvation, including those who die of disease, abuse, starvation, and warfare, does get us to quite a large portion of humanity. Still, that large total falls short of "the vast majority of the whole mass of humanity," and I don't see how we get to that larger number without including huge numbers of adult human beings who have died without ever hearing the gospel proclaimed.

I can't imagine that at least some of them had conversations on the subject, and came to agreement that it was an estimate they could defend. I wish we had a record of those conversations.

I also have questions about why Kuyper was so convinced of the small-number view. His close colleague Bavinck was certainly given to an expansive understanding of the end time:

> The state of glory, Scripture tells us, will be rich and splendid beyond all description. We look for a new heaven, a new earth, a new humanity, a restored universe, an ever-progressing development never again disturbed by sin. To that end, the creation and the fall, Adam and Christ, nature and grace, faith and unbelief, election and reprobation—all work together, each in its own way, not only consequently but in concert. Indeed, even the present world, along with its history, is as such already an ongoing revelation of God's perfections. It will continue to exert its influence in depth and in breadth also in the coming dispensation, and to furnish a new humanity with ever new reasons for the worship and glorification of God.[3]

3. Herman Bavinck, *Reformed Dogmatics*, ed. John Bolt, trans. John Vriend, vol. 2 (Grand Rapids: Baker Academic, 2004), 391–92.

The expansive language here would seem to be the kind we can imagine Kuyper also using. I wonder too whether the two of them ever talked about these things.

The Westminster Confession certainly removes any serious obstacle to accepting the majoritarian vision by offering its own marvelously expansive depiction of the Holy Spirit's regenerating ministry. He "worketh when, and where, and how he pleaseth"—thus allowing, as A. A. Hodge recognized, that persons may be "regenerated and sanctified immediately by God *without the use of means.*"

In the Calvinist community that formed me, I did sometimes hear things that pointed in the direction of a large-number scenario without actually arriving there theologically. This typically occurred for me on family occasions when someone would raise a question about a specific person. I remember my Dutch Reformed aunt speaking glowingly about her neighbor. "We have great conversations about things, and we often agree. It makes me wonder because she is a Polish Catholic—but often she actually sounds Christian!" Then someone else would remark (and this would usually end the conversation with heads nodding in agreement), "Well, you never know. Sometimes I think that when we get to heaven we will be surprised by who else is there!"

At its heart Calvinism is a theology of surprises. This is why even its gloomier expressions can serve to celebrate in our souls the wonders of sovereign grace:

> Alas, and did my Savior bleed
> And did my Sov'reign die?
> Would He devote that sacred head
> For such a worm as I?

And this experience of surprise in our deep places prepares us to be open to see God's mercies reaching into the deep places of others—and even to more cosmic surprises. God so loved the world—the *kosmos*, the creation that in the beginning God declared to be good—that he sent the Son into our midst so that the whole creation could be saved and renewed through his redemptive mission. Then the risen and ascended Lord sent his Spirit to call an elect people into being, to bring divine blessings to all the nations of the earth. What the final nature and scope of those blessings will be brings the promise that great surprises are yet to come, by the power of the Spirit, who "worketh when, and where, and how he pleaseth."

Index